everyday
little cakes

everyday
little ∨ cakes

**50+ PERFECTLY PROPORTIONED CONFECTIONS
TO ENJOY ANY DAY OF THE WEEK**

CANDACE
FLOYD

SPRING HOUSE PRESS

Text © 2018 by Candace Floyd
Photographs © 2018 by Danielle Atkins

The opinions expressed in this book are the author's own and do not necessarily reflect the views of Spring House Press.

Publisher: Paul McGahren
Editorial Director: Matthew Teague
Copy Editor: Kerri Grzybicki
Design: Lindsay Hess
Layout: Jodie Delohery
Photography: Danielle Atkins
Photo Styling: Teresa Blackburn
Indexer: Jay Kreider

Spring House Press
P.O. Box 239
Whites Creek, TN 37189

ISBN: 978-1-940611-67-9
Library of Congress Control Number: 2018935590

Printed in China

10 9 8 7 6 5 4 3 2 1

Note: The following list contains names used in *Little Everyday Cakes* that may be registered with the United States Copyright Office: Bailey's Irish Cream; Cortland; Fat Daddio's; Ford (Model T); Fostoria; Grandma's Original Molasses; Granny Smith; Hostess; Jack Daniel's; Julia Child; Little Debbie; *Mastering the Art of French Cooking; Nashville Seasons;* Parrish Magic Line; The Junior League of Nashville; Whisper Creek Tennessee Sipping Cream; Whoppers; and Wilton.

Pictured recipes: Front cover: 88. Page 2, from top left to bottom right: 74, 90, 110, 100, 28, 82, 98. Page 4: 70. Back cover, from top left to bottom right: 130, 28, 70, 56.

To learn more about Spring House Press books, or to find a retailer near you, email info@springhousepress.com or visit us at www.springhousepress.com.

acknowledgments

Want to make some new friends? Write a cake cookbook and test every single recipe in your kitchen in six months' time!

So many friends and family members helped me with the recipe development, testing, and tinkering. Thanks to number one taster and super-duper friend-for-life Eva Elliott, who offered great suggestions and whisked me away to lunch whenever I needed a break. Also thanks to my dear sisters-in-law, Susan Glasgow Brown and Emily Glasgow Bruno, and aunt Suzanne Brimm Moore, for tasting, critiquing, and for supplying me with ideas for recipes.

The crew at Spring House Press—editorial director Matthew Teague, publisher Paul McGahren, copyeditor Kerri Grzybicki, designer Lindsay Hess, and layout artist Jodie Delohery—were a dream to work with. You couldn't ask for a better team of publishing pros.

This book would be far less lovely without the help of my photo stylist and friend of more than ten years, Teresa Blackburn, who never ceases to amaze me with her sense of style, great taste, and wise advice. Thanks as well to my new friend Danielle Atkins, whose photographs in this book truly take the cake! Her grace and patience made our marathon three-day photo session a breeze.

And to Bim Glasgow, husband, encourager, taster, and partner in all manner of adventures, you're the best ever. I love you the most, times infinity.

contents

80

92

84

78

introduction

Make a little cake.
Every day deserves a treat.

Ask most any home cook, and you'll find they're more of a pie or cookie baker than a cake baker. I used to be that way too. I've always loved cake, especially the Citrus Cake (page 70) my mother made for my birthday every year (and mailed to me while I was away at college), the "Yellow" Butter Cake (page 110) with chocolate icing she made for my younger brother's birthday, and my great-grandmother's Jam Cake (page 40) that was part of every Christmas season. But for me and for most home cooks, the problem with cake is, well, there's just too much of it—unless you're taking it to a potluck or have a family of ten. To me, leftover cake just looks sad. It's no longer that pristine iced confection you can't wait to cut into. It's been spoiled.

That's why I decided to explore "little" cakes. Making just enough for a family of four or five to enjoy, little cakes don't present the leftover problem. And if you do have some remaining, they're easy to cover right in the pan or transfer to a storage container. If they need to be chilled, they're short enough to fit in the refrigerator without rearranging all the shelves.

In short (ha!), little cakes are perfect packages of yumminess and ease.

I first came to see the beauty of "little" cakes as a young child visiting my grandparents. My grandmother, Lucy Catherine Hazzard Brimm (called "Queen" by most everyone she knew, "Queenie" by her Floyd grandchildren, and "Miss Queen" by her son-in-law, my father), was a wizard in the kitchen. For special occasions, this lady from the most rural area of Middle Tennessee you can imagine could please even sophisticated tastes. Sweet potatoes were pureed and stuffed into hollowed-out orange rinds, green beans were served in china bowls (*never* glass), the table was set with china and silver and her beloved Fostoria glasses, and desserts were towering affairs, like Vanilla Sponge Cake with Pineapple Filling and Caramel Frosting (page 108). She knew, though, that even a weeknight with family (and grandchildren) needed a cake. That's when she would bake a little cake. Our favorites were One Egg Dinner Cake (page 24) served with sliced peaches and ice cream, Black Pudding (page 26) topped with sliced bananas and warm Butter Sauce (page 144), and Fresh Apple Cake (page 62) with warm Lemon Butter Sauce (page 145).

Little cakes were just big enough for the family to polish off in one sitting. Leftovers didn't linger, needing a place to be stored and serving as a reminder of wasted ingredients.

That no-waste aspect surely appealed to Queenie. Born in 1900, she spent her early twenties as a flapper tooling around the countryside in a Model T Ford. By 1925, though, she was married and starting a family. By the end of the Depression, she had five children (two more followed in the 1940s). Frugality was a necessity.

Like most who lived through the Depression, she never lost her no-waste mindset. Little cakes were there to stay, and her grandchildren, who started coming along in the 1950s, were the happy beneficiaries.

This book honors Queenie and her six daughters—all masters of baking, cooking, making do with what they have, filling hungry stomachs, and surprising little children with a tasty little cake.

getting started

Making little cakes isn't just a matter of dividing the ingredients for a standard layer cake or sheet cake in half. Scaling down a recipe turns into a head-scratcher when the original calls for three eggs or one-third cup of this or that. Cooking temperatures, cooking times, and leavening amounts all change with the volume of the batter.

The guesswork is gone with the cakes in this book, all of which have been tinkered with, adjusted, tested, and tasted so that each perfectly fills its baking pan and gets done in the time provided.

Some of the cakes in this book are traditionally made as "little" cakes. Known as snack cakes, they slice up into small squares or wedges that are perfect for toting to work or school in a lunch bag. The chapter on fruit-flavored cakes includes recipes that take full advantage of seasonal fruit, with their moist, sweet fillings and tart sauce toppings. Others are little cake iterations of full-blown glories we all love—Hummingbird Cake, Maple Cake, and "Yellow" Butter Cake. The cakes in the Shrinking Act chapter rein in the overblown size of these beauties, making just enough for a night or two. A group of upside down cakes and cakes flavored with alcohol, like rum and whiskey, are festive and fabulous—great for anniversary celebrations and more. A collection of breakfast cakes will make you want to start your day with a small bit of sweetness.

weights and measures

How do commercial bakers get such consistent results in texture? They don't use measuring cups; instead, all the ingredients are weighed. Small scales for home use are inexpensive and available at any cookware store, and I highly recommend buying one and using it for all your baking recipes.

The recipes in this book include both the volume (cup measure) and weights in grams for ingredients whose weights matter—flour, sugar, butter and oil, milks, and chocolate. For consistent results, opt for measuring these ingredients by weight instead of volume. Flour weight can vary enormously according to how the flour is measured: dipping a cup into a bin of flour often results in a higher weight than lightly spooning flour into a cup and leveling it off with a knife. If a cake has too much flour, it will be dense and rubbery.

For flavorings, like vanilla extract and salt, and leavening, like baking powder and baking soda, amounts are provided in teaspoons as any variation you might get from slightly over- or under-filling the spoon is insignificant. For the leavening, make sure your baking powder and baking soda have not passed their expiration date.

All the recipes in this book use large eggs rather than small or extra large. Sometimes an extra egg yolk is called for: this helps tenderize the cake and keep it moist.

STANDARD WEIGHTS FOR INGREDIENTS

All-purpose flour	1 cup	120g
Sugar, granulated	1 cup	198g
Sugar, confectioner's	1 cup	114g
Sugar, brown	1 cup packed	213g
Egg, whole		49g
Egg yolk		14g
Egg white		35g
Milk	1 cup	227g
Butter	1 tablespoon	14g
	½ cup	113g
Buttermilk	½ cup	113g
	1 cup	225g
Sour cream or yogurt	1 cup	243g
Heavy cream	1 cup	238g
Chocolate, roughly chopped	1 cup	120g
Chocolate chips	1 cup	160g
Cocoa powder	1 cup	120g
Oil	1 cup	198g

Opt for measuring certain ingredients by weight, rather than by volume, to get consistent results. Inexpensive scales are available at most cookware stores.

pans

For most of the cakes in this book, you won't need any special pans or equipment. The majority are made in standard 8-inch square or round cake pans or loaf pans (8½ by 4½ inches). For special occasions, like small birthday celebrations or anniversary dinners at home, you might turn to the cakes made in two 6-inch round pans and then layered. The pans used in this book are made by Fat Daddio's, Wilton, Parrish's Magic Line, and others and are available in stores and through many online retailers.

For the best results, use the size and shape pan called for in the recipe. The volume of an 8-inch square pan (128 cubic inches) is significantly higher than the volume of an 8-inch round pan (100.5 cubic inches); batter amounts, the height of the finished cake, and cooking times will be different for the two different shapes.

The best cake pans are sturdy, with straight sides and a depth of 2 inches. Lighter colored pans are best, as they won't overbrown the edges. Look for pans made of 16-gauge uncoated anodized aluminum. Rolled edges help prevent warping.

techniques used in this book

BUTTER CAKES

These cakes are tender, moist, and fine-grained, and their technique is familiar to most: Beat the softened butter with an electric mixer until creamy. Add the sugar, and beat at medium-high speed for 4 or 5 minutes. This beats air into the butter, which helps give cakes their lift. These cakes are also called high-ratio cakes, because of the ratio of sugar to flour. The weight of the sugar is always equal to or greater than the weight of the flour. In addition, the weight of the eggs is equal to the weight of the fat. And the weight of the liquid (the eggs and milk) is equal to (or slightly greater than) the weight of the sugar. Note that we're talking about weight here—not volume.

POUND CAKES

The formula for pound cakes is super easy. The weights of the flour, eggs, fat, and sugar are equal. The result is a moist, soft, rich cake that's somewhat dense in texture.

SPONGE CAKES

Somewhat firm but still delicate, sponge cakes are sometimes called genoise—named for the Italian city of Genoa. Without any leavening (or very little), these cakes get their rise from egg yolks that are beaten until fully aerated. Sometimes the eggs and sugar are warmed in a double boiler before beating, but not in all cases. Next, the egg whites are beaten separately until soft peaks form. It's important to remember that the bowl and beaters need to be spotlessly clean and dry before beating egg whites. Even a trace of oil on the beaters or in the bowl can result in whites that don't fluff as much as they should. Once the whites are softly peaked, they're gently folded in with the egg yolks along with the flour. If butter is used, it's melted first, then cooled, then folded into the batter.

SIFTING

Today's flours are much more finely ground than the flours your mother or grandmother used. I'm lazy, and I'll admit: I don't sift my flour. I've found that spooning the flour into a bowl, adding the leaveners and salt, and tossing lightly with a wire whisk is typically sufficient to lighten the flour. For cocoa powder and confectioner's sugar, sifting is needed. If you don't have a sifter, place the ingredient in a wire mesh sieve and tap it against your hand, letting the powder fall into a bowl.

CREAMING

The process of beating butter and sugar and sometimes eggs until a creamy, fluffy mass is created, creaming adds air bubbles to the mixture, which help baked goods rise. Baking powder added to the mixture enlarges the air bubbles. Creaming takes time—count on beating butter and sugar with an electric mixer at medium-high speed for 4 or 5 minutes.

FOLDING

The process of gently blending one ingredient into another, folding is a technique used to maintain air bubbles created by beating. Typically recipes that use beaten egg whites call for them to be folded into the batter. The best way to fold is to spoon a third of the lighter ingredient (like beaten egg whites) into the heavy mixture (the batter base), then run a rubber spatula down the sides of the bowl, draw it toward the middle and then pull it up. Turn the bowl a quarter turn, and repeat the running and drawing motions. Keep turning and drawing up until blended. Then repeat the process twice with the remaining lighter ingredients.

A rubber spatula works well in folding beaten egg whites into a batter. Don't be too forceful in your folding motions to avoid deflating the egg whites.

Less expensive than butter, vegetable shortening is perfectly suited for greasing cake pans.

PREPARING THE PAN

Vegetable shortening works perfectly for greasing cake pans. Be sure to get the shortening into the corners and cover the bottom of the pan evenly. Also grease the sides up to about ½ inch from the top of the pan. Next, spoon a tablespoon or two of flour into the pan. If you're making a chocolate cake, use unsweetened cocoa powder instead of flour to keep the cake brown. Tap the sides of the pan to scatter the flour over the greased bottom. Then tilt the pan to scatter the flour up the greased sides. Turn the pan upside down, and tap to remove excess flour.

Some recipes call for lining the pan with parchment. Place the pan on a sheet of parchment, and trace around the edge with a pencil. Set the pan aside, and cut out the traced shape with scissors. Then grease the pan as described above. Place the parchment into the pan, and grease the parchment. Then dust the pan with flour as described above.

A parchment paper liner helps release the baked cakes from their pans.

TESTING FOR DONENESS

Wooden toothpicks, skinny wooden skewers, or clean broom straws make great cake testers. Insert the pick into the cake at the center, then remove. If the tester comes out dry or with moist crumbs, the cake is done. Another test is to press the top of the cake in the center lightly with your fingertips. If it springs back, the cake is done. Also watch for the cake to pull away from the sides of the pan. For sponge cakes, you can test the cake for doneness by placing your fingertips on the edge of the cake, then slighting pulling the cake away from the side of the pan.

To test for doneness, lightly press the top of the cake in the center. If it springs back to the touch, it's done (above). Or insert a wooden cake tester or clean broom straw into the center of the cake and remove. If it comes out clean or with moist crumbs attached, the cake is done (right).

To allow air to circulate around the cake as it cools, place the pan on a wire rack.

COOLING

Wire racks allow air to circulate around the cake. Most cakes need to cool in their pans in order to set. The time varies from 10 to 20 minutes, depending on the recipe. Don't let the cake cool completely in the pan, however, if you're planning to remove it. It will release from the pan best if it is still warm. Some snack cakes can be left in place and frosted or glazed right in the pan.

REMOVING

Once the cake has cooled for the specified amount of time in the pan, place a plate or wire rack over the pan. Turn the cake upside down, and gently pull away the pan. Sometimes a firm rap or two may be needed. If you've lined the pan with parchment, peel the paper away. Return the cake, top side up, to the wire rack to cool completely.

ICING

While the tops of some cakes are iced in the pan, others are removed to a cake plate first so that the sides can be iced as well. To keep the plate clean, place strips of parchment or waxed paper under the cake to cover the plate. Using an offset spatula, ice the sides, then move to the top. For layered cakes, place one layer on the cake plate, ice the sides and top, then place the second layer on top and ice the sides and top. Use about one third of the frosting for the bottom layer and its sides and the remaining frosting for the top layer and

Use an offset spatula to frost the baked cake. It's much easier to create frosting whirls with these tools than with a plain butter knife.

sides. A small offset spatula allows you to create beautiful whirls in the frosting. Once you're finished, gently pull the paper strips out and discard.

If your cake layers have formed a dome while baking, you'll need to level off at least the bottom layer. Use a serrated bread knife to cut off the domed portion. Then ice the cake as described earlier.

STORING

A variety of cake boxes are available—from plastic storage containers to glass cake domes. Whatever you decide to use, keep your cakes covered or securely wrapped in plastic wrap or foil so they don't dry out.

1

snack cakes

· · · · · · · · · · ·

Move over, Little Debbie and Hostess. Here are some homemade snack cakes that will make you stand up and pay attention!

Typically made in an 8- or 9-inch square pan or an 8- or 9-inch round pan, snack cakes are cut into squares or wedges for serving. They sport glazes, full-blown icings, or a dusting of confectioner's sugar. A few are even left bare and are beautiful all on their own. You'll get nine servings from a square snack cake when making two cuts in each direction or eight servings from a round cake when cut into wedges—enough for a family of four to have for an after-dinner treat and lunch the next day.

· · · · · · · · · · ·

one egg dinner cake

SERVES 8

*H*ere's the cake that started my fascination with little cakes. My grandmother Queenie made this often and served it in a variety of ways—with sliced fresh peaches and ice cream, with strawberries and Sweetened Whipped Cream, or with Fudgy Chocolate Sauce.

2 cups all-purpose flour (240g)

3 teaspoons baking powder

½ teaspoon salt

½ cup unsalted butter, softened (113g)

1 cup granulated sugar (198g)

1 egg, room temperature

1 teaspoon vanilla extract

¾ cup whole milk, room temperature (170g)

1 tablespoon coarse sugar (optional)

Preheat the oven to 350°F (180°C). Grease a 9-inch round cake pan. Line the bottom with parchment paper, and grease the parchment. Dust the pan with flour.

Whisk together the flour, baking powder, and salt in a small bowl.

Place the butter in a mixing bowl, and beat with an electric mixer at medium-high speed until creamy. Add the granulated sugar, and beat until fluffy, about 5 minutes. Add the egg and vanilla, and beat until well combined. Reduce the speed to low, and add the flour mixture and milk a little at a time, beginning and ending with the flour mixture. Beat until just smooth. Scrape into the prepared pan.

Bake the cake 25 to 30 minutes, until golden brown and a tester inserted in the center comes out clean. Place the pan on a wire rack, and let the cake cool 15 minutes. Turn the cake out of the pan, and return it to the rack, top side up. Sprinkle the coarse sugar on top, if using, and let the cake cool completely.

Cut the cake into wedges, and serve with sliced fruit or berries, ice cream, Sweetened Whipped Cream (page 151), or Fudgy Chocolate Sauce (page 149).

black pudding

SERVES 9

In England and Ireland, black pudding is a type of blood sausage. Don't worry—that's not what this is. This cake is best served warm. Leftovers are a disappointment, but that shouldn't be a problem. There's no need to cut this cake into squares. Simply scoop out servings with a large spoon, and place them in a bowl.

Preheat the oven to 350°F (180°C). Grease an 8-inch square cake pan, and dust the pan with cocoa powder.

Whisk together the flour, salt, baking powder, and cocoa in a medium bowl. Pour the buttermilk in a measuring cup, and stir in the baking soda. Place the butter in a mixing bowl, and beat with an electric mixer at medium-high speed until creamy. Add the sugar, and beat until fluffy, about 5 minutes. Reduce the speed to low, and add the flour mixture and buttermilk mixture a little at a time, beginning and ending with the flour mixture. Beat until just smooth. Add the vanilla, and beat 30 seconds. The batter will be very thick. Scrape the batter into the prepared pan, and smooth the top.

Bake the cake 20 to 25 minutes, until a tester inserted in the cake comes out with moist crumbs attached and the cake begins to pull away from the sides of the pan.

Scoop servings of the cake into a bowl, and serve topped with the Butter Sauce, banana slices, and ice cream.

cake

2 cups all-purpose flour (240g)

½ teaspoon salt

¼ teaspoon baking powder

7 tablespoons unsweetened cocoa powder (53g)

1 cup buttermilk, room temperature (225g)

1 teaspoon baking soda

¼ cup unsalted butter, softened (56g)

¾ cup sugar (150g)

1 teaspoon vanilla extract

topping

Butter Sauce (page 144)

Bananas, sliced

Ice cream

almond-coffee cake

SERVES 8

Based on Julia Child's almond cake in *Mastering the Art of French Cooking*, this sponge cake is super light with a heady kick of coffee flavoring. Sprinkle with confectioner's sugar or drizzle with Chocolate Glaze. A shower of toasted almonds makes it smashing.

Preheat the oven to 350°F (180°C). Grease an 8-inch round cake pan. Line the bottom with parchment paper, and grease the parchment. Dust the pan with flour.

Place ¾ cup of the almonds and 3 tablespoons of the sugar in the bowl of a food processor. Process until the almonds are finely ground.

Place the egg yolks in a mixing bowl, and beat with an electric mixer at medium speed until smooth. Add the remaining ½ cup (99g) sugar, and beat until thick and pale, about 4 minutes.

Add the almond mixture to the yolk mixture along with the almond extract, espresso powder, and coffee. Beat on low speed until blended.

In a separate bowl using clean, dry beaters, beat the egg whites until foamy. Add the salt, and continue beating on high speed until soft peaks form. Using a rubber spatula, stir one-quarter of the egg whites into the almond mixture until blended. Gently fold in one-third of the remaining egg whites and one-third of the flour. Repeat twice. Gently fold in the cooled butter. (Do not overmix or you will deflate the egg whites.) Pour the batter into the prepared pan. It should come to within ¼-inch from the top.

Bake the cake 25 to 30 minutes. The cake is done when it springs back when lightly pressed on the top and when you can pull the edges away from the sides of the pan with your fingertips.

Place the pan on a wire rack, and let the cake cool 20 minutes. Run a small knife around the inside of the pan. Remove the cake from the pan, and return it, top side up, to the rack to cool completely.

Drizzle the top of the cake with Chocolate Glaze, and sprinkle with the toasted almonds, or simply dust with confectioner's sugar. Cut into wedges to serve.

¾ cup blanched almonds, plus ¼ cup, toasted, for topping

½ cup plus 3 tablespoons sugar, divided (99g + 37g)

3 eggs, room temperature, separated

¼ teaspoon almond extract

2 teaspoons instant espresso powder

¼ cup brewed coffee, room temperature (59g)

Pinch of salt

½ cup all-purpose flour (60g)

3 tablespoons unsalted butter, melted and cooled (42g)

Chocolate Glaze, optional (page 145)

chocolate snack cake

SERVES 9

*S*prinkle this super moist, rich chocolate cake with confectioner's sugar when cool, or top with Easy Chocolate Buttercream Frosting or Peanut Butter Frosting.

Preheat the oven to 350°F (180°C). Grease an 8-inch square cake pan, and dust with cocoa powder.

Whisk together the flour, sugar, baking soda, salt, and cocoa in a large bowl.

Place the egg in small bowl, and whisk lightly. Add the vanilla, vinegar, water, and oil, and whisk until blended. Pour over the flour mixture, and whisk until smooth. The batter will be thin. Pour the batter into the prepared pan.

Bake the cake 20 to 25 minutes, until a tester inserted in the center comes out almost clean. Place the pan on a wire rack, and let the cake cool completely.

Dust the cooled cake with confectioner's sugar, or top, while in the pan, with the frosting of your choice.

1½ cups all-purpose flour (180g)

1 cup sugar (198g)

1 teaspoon baking soda

½ teaspoon salt

3 tablespoons unsweetened cocoa powder (23g)

1 egg, room temperature, slightly beaten

1 tablespoon vanilla extract

1 tablespoon white vinegar

1 cup warm water

6 tablespoons canola oil (74g)

Easy Chocolate Buttercream Frosting (page 148) or Peanut Butter Frosting (page 148)

fudge cake with cherries and pecans

SERVES 9

My mother-in-law, Bobbie Glasgow, introduced me to One Pan Fudge Cake, included in The Junior League of Nashville's *Nashville Seasons* cookbook. It's a dream to put together—no mixer needed. My version is tricked up with pecans and dried cherries.

Preheat the oven to 325°F (165°C). Grease an 8-inch square cake pan.

Place the butter, chocolate, and granulated sugar in the top of a double boiler, and melt over barely simmering water, stirring occasionally, until smooth. Remove from heat. Sift in the flour, baking powder, and salt. Stir until well combined. Stir in the eggs and vanilla until blended. Stir in the pecans and cherries. Spoon the batter into the prepared pan.

Bake the cake 25 to 30 minutes, until the cake begins to pull away from the sides and a tester inserted in the center comes out almost clean. Place the pan on a wire rack, and let the cake cool slightly. Cut the cake into squares while still warm, but leave it in the pan. Let the cake cool completely, and dust with confectioner's sugar.

½ cup unsalted butter (113g)

1½ ounces unsweetened chocolate (43g)

1 cup granulated sugar (198g)

¾ cup all-purpose flour (90g)

¼ teaspoon baking powder

1 teaspoon salt

2 eggs, room temperature, slightly beaten

1 teaspoon vanilla extract

1 cup chopped pecans

½ cup dried cherries, halved

Confectioner's sugar

honey-ginger sour cream cake

SERVES 9

*T*he old-timer's cold and flu remedy—honey, lemon juice, and ginger—perfectly bakes up in a snack cake.

Preheat the oven to 325°F (165°C). Grease an 8-inch square cake pan, and dust the pan with flour.

Whisk together the flour, baking powder, baking soda, salt, and ginger in a small bowl.

Place the butter in a mixing bowl, and beat with an electric mixer at medium-high speed until creamy. Add the sugar, and beat until fluffy, about 4 minutes. Add ½ cup of the honey, and beat until smooth. Add the eggs one at a time, beating after each addition. The batter may look curdled, but it will come together when the flour is added. Add the flour mixture and sour cream a little at a time, beginning and ending with the flour mixture. Beat until just blended. Add half the lemon juice and lemon peel, and beat 30 seconds. Pour the batter into the prepared cake pan.

Bake the cake 35 to 40 minutes, until a tester inserted in the center comes out clean and the top of the cake is deep golden brown. Place the pan on a wire rack, and let the cake cool 10 minutes. As the cake cools, it will slightly shrink in width and height. You can leave the cake in the pan or remove it—your choice.

Place the remaining 3 tablespoons of the honey and the remaining lemon juice in a glass measuring cup. Microwave 15 seconds. Stir well. Add the vanilla and the remaining lemon peel, and stir well.

Spread the glaze over the top of the cake with the back of a spoon. Cut the cake into squares.

1¼ cups all-purpose flour (150g)

1¼ teaspoons baking powder

½ teaspoon baking soda

½ teaspoon salt

1 teaspoon ground ginger

½ cup unsalted butter, softened (113g)

½ cup sugar (99g)

½ cup plus 3 tablespoons honey, divided (340g + 64g)

2 eggs, room temperature

¾ cup sour cream, room temperature (182g)

2 tablespoons lemon juice, divided

1 teaspoon finely grated lemon peel, divided

1 teaspoon vanilla extract

earl gray tea cake

SERVES 9

The milk used in this cake, a riff on the popular coffee shop beverage called London Fog, is infused with Earl Gray tea.

Heat the milk in a small saucepan over medium heat until small bubbles begin to appear around the edge of the pan. Remove the pan from the heat, and add 3 of the teabags. Let stand 15 minutes. Remove the teabags, squeezing each to release the liquid. Let the milk cool to room temperature.

Preheat the oven to 325°F (165°C). Grease an 8-inch square cake pan, and dust the pan with flour.

Whisk together the flour, baking powder, and salt in a medium bowl.

Place the butter in a mixing bowl, and beat with an electric mixer at medium-high speed until creamy. Add the granulated sugar, and beat until fluffy, about 4 minutes. Add the eggs, one at a time, beating well after each addition. Reduce the speed to low, and add the flour mixture and ½ cup of the milk-tea a little at a time, beginning and ending with the flour mixture. Beat until just smooth. Add the lemon peel and vanilla, and beat 30 seconds. Pour the batter into the prepared pan.

Bake the cake 22 to 25 minutes, until a tester inserted in the center comes out clean and the top of the cake is deep golden brown. Place the pan on a wire rack, and let the cake cool 10 minutes. Remove the cake from the pan, and return it, top side up, to the rack to cool completely.

Pour the boiling water over the remaining tea bag. Let stand 5 minutes. Remove the tea bag, squeezing it to release the liquid.

Combine 3 tablespoons of the brewed tea with the confectioner's sugar in a small bowl, and whisk until smooth. Spoon the glaze over the cooled cake.

cake

⅔ cup whole milk (150g)

3 Earl Gray tea bags

1½ cups all-purpose flour (180g)

1½ teaspoons baking powder

½ teaspoon salt

7 tablespoons unsalted butter, softened (98g)

1 cup granulated sugar (198g)

2 eggs, room temperature

1 teaspoon finely grated lemon peel

1 teaspoon vanilla extract

glaze

¼ cup boiling water

1 Earl Gray tea bag

¾ cup confectioner's sugar, sifted

gingerbread cake

SERVES 9

No mixer needed for this super tender gingerbread that includes a bit of whole-wheat flour to give it more texture. It's made with buttermilk instead of the more traditional hot water.

Preheat the oven to 350°F (180°C). Butter an 8-inch square cake pan, and dust the pan with flour.

Whisk together the flours, granulated sugar, baking soda, salt, ginger, cinnamon, cloves, and nutmeg in a large bowl.

Combine the butter and molasses in a small bowl. Stir until well blended. Pour over the flour mixture, and stir until smooth. Add the water, and stir until smooth. Combine the egg and buttermilk in a small bowl, and whisk until blended. Pour into the batter, and stir until blended. The batter will be thin. Pour the batter into the prepared pan.

Bake the cake 20 to 25 minutes, until a tester inserted in the center comes out clean. Sprinkle the coarse sugar on top. Place the pan on a wire rack, and let the cake cool about 10 minutes. The cake is best served warm with Sweetened Whipped Cream.

¾ cup all-purpose flour (90g)

¾ cup whole wheat flour (85g)

3 tablespoons granulated sugar (37g)

¾ teaspoon baking soda

½ teaspoon salt

1¼ teaspoons ground ginger

¾ teaspoon ground cinnamon

⅛ teaspoon ground cloves

⅛ teaspoon ground nutmeg

6 tablespoons unsalted butter, melted and cooled (84g)

½ cup molasses, like Grandma's Original, not blackstrap (170g)

3 tablespoons water (42g)

1 egg, room temperature

⅔ cup buttermilk, room temperature (148g)

2 teaspoons coarse sugar

Sweetened Whipped Cream (page 151), optional

jam cake

SERVES 9

This recipe is based on one from my great-grandmother, Granny Brimm. It's a perfect showcase for homemade Caramel Frosting.

Preheat the oven to 325°F (165°C). Grease an 8-inch square cake pan. Line with parchment paper. Grease the parchment. Dust the pan with flour.

Whisk together the flour, salt, allspice, cloves, and cinnamon in a small bowl.

Combine the buttermilk and baking soda in a small bowl.

Place the butter in a mixing bowl, and using an electric mixer at medium-high speed, beat until creamy. Add the sugar, and beat until fluffy, about 4 minutes. Add the eggs and egg yolk one at a time, beating well after each addition. Reduce the speed to low, and add the flour mixture and the buttermilk mixture a little at a time, beginning and ending with the flour mixture. Fold in the jam and pecans. Scrape the batter into the prepared pan.

Bake the cake 35 to 40 minutes, until a tester inserted in the center comes out clean. Place the pan on a wire rack, and let the cake cool 10 minutes. Remove the cake from the pan, and return it, top side up, to the rack to cool completely. Frost the top of the cake with Caramel Frosting.

1½ cups all-purpose flour (180g)

½ teaspoon salt

½ teaspoon ground allspice

½ teaspoon ground cloves

¼ teaspoon ground cinnamon

9 tablespoons buttermilk, room temperature (126g)

½ teaspoon baking soda

½ cup unsalted butter, softened (113g)

1 cup sugar (198g)

2 eggs, room temperature

1 egg yolk, room temperature

½ cup blackberry jam or preserves

½ cup chopped pecans

½ recipe Caramel Frosting (page 146)

marble cake

SERVES 9

This cake is so pretty it doesn't need a frosting, but you may want to top it with a dollop of Sweetened Whipped Cream (page 151) or a scoop of vanilla ice cream to serve.

Preheat the oven to 350°F (180°C). Grease an 8-inch square cake pan. Line with parchment paper. Grease the parchment. Dust the pan with flour.

Whisk together the flour, baking powder, and salt in a small bowl.

Place the butter in a mixing bowl, and using an electric mixer at medium-high speed, beat until creamy. Add the sugar, and beat until fluffy, about 4 minutes. Add the eggs and egg yolk one at a time, beating well after each addition. Add the flour mixture and all but 1 tablespoon of the milk a little at a time, beginning and ending with the flour mixture. Beat until just smooth. Add the vanilla, and beat 30 seconds.

Spoon about half the batter into the prepared pan, creating about five separate dollops. To the remaining batter, add the cocoa and the remaining 1 tablespoon of the milk, and stir until blended. Spoon the chocolate batter in between the dollops of vanilla batter. Using a butter knife, swirl the batters together.

Bake the cake 20 to 25 minutes, until a tester inserted in the center comes out clean. Place the pan on a wire rack, and let the cake cool in the pan. Serve directly from the pan or invert onto a cake plate.

1½ cups all-purpose flour (180g)

1¼ teaspoons baking powder

½ teaspoon salt

9 tablespoons unsalted butter, softened (127g)

¾ cup sugar (149g)

2 eggs, room temperature

1 egg yolk, room temperature

¾ cup whole milk, room temperature (170g)

1½ teaspoons vanilla extract

3 tablespoons unsweetened cocoa powder (23g)

peanut butter snack cake

SERVES 9

If you have peanut butter lovers in your house, this is the cake for you. You can let the cake cool in the pan and frost it without turning it out, making this cake a cinch to pack up for picnics or potlucks. Use the Peanut Butter Frosting or Easy Chocolate Buttercream to top this tender cake.

Preheat the oven to 350°F (180°C). Grease an 8-inch square cake pan, and dust the pan with flour.

Combine the peanut butter and oil in a small saucepan. Heat over medium heat, stirring constantly, until peanut butter melts and the mixture is smooth.

Whisk together the egg, buttermilk, and vanilla in a small bowl.

Combine the flour, baking powder, baking soda, salt, and brown sugar in a mixing bowl. Using an electric mixer on low speed, mix for 30 seconds. Add the egg mixture, and beat on low speed until almost blended. Gradually add the peanut butter mixture, and beat until just smooth. Pour the batter into the prepared pan.

Bake the cake 18 to 20 minutes, until a tester inserted in the center comes out clean. Place the pan on a wire rack, and let the cake cool completely.

Spread the frosting of your choice on top of the cake in the pan. Scatter the chopped peanuts on top. Refrigerate the cake until the frosting hardens a bit, about 20 minutes.

3 tablespoons creamy peanut butter (not natural peanut butter)

3 tablespoons canola oil (37g)

1 egg, room temperature

½ cup buttermilk, room temperature (117g)

½ teaspoon vanilla extract

1¼ cups all-purpose flour (150g)

1¼ teaspoons baking powder

¼ teaspoon baking soda

¼ teaspoon salt

¾ cup packed brown sugar (159g)

Peanut Butter Frosting (page 148) or Easy Chocolate Buttercream Frosting (page 148)

⅓ cup chopped honey-roasted peanuts

pumpkin pound cake loaf

SERVES 8

M ade in a loaf pan, this little cake slices up perfectly for lunch portions. The unfrosted loaf freezes well, wrapped in foil and placed in a freezer bag.

Preheat the oven to 300°F (150°C). Grease an 8½ by 4½-inch loaf pan. Dust the pan with flour.

Whisk together the flour, baking powder, baking soda, salt, cinnamon, nutmeg, and cloves in medium bowl.

Place the butter in a mixing bowl, and using an electric mixer, beat on medium-high speed until creamy. Gradually add the sugars, and beat until fluffy, about 4 minutes. Add the eggs one at a time, beating after each addition. Add the pumpkin and vanilla, and beat until combined. Reduce the speed to low, and add the flour mixture and buttermilk a little at a time, beginning and ending with the flour mixture. Spoon the batter into prepared pan.

Bake the cake 50 to 55 minutes, until a tester inserted in the center comes out clean. Place the pan on a wire rack, and let the cake cool 10 minutes. Remove the cake from the pan, and return it, top side up, to the rack to cool completely.

If frosting the cake, spread Cream Cheese Frosting on top of the cake. Scatter toasted walnuts or pecans on top.

1½ cups all-purpose flour (180g)

½ teaspoon baking powder

½ teaspoon baking soda

½ teaspoon salt

1 teaspoon ground cinnamon

¼ teaspoon ground nutmeg

¼ teaspoon ground cloves

¼ cup unsalted butter, softened (56g)

½ cup granulated sugar (99g)

¼ cup packed brown sugar (53g)

2 eggs, room temperature

1 cup canned pure pumpkin (244g)

½ teaspoon vanilla extract

6 tablespoons buttermilk, room temperature (84g)

½ recipe Cream Cheese Frosting, optional (page 144)

Chopped walnuts or pecans, toasted, optional

pumpkin spice cake
with COCONUT TOPPING

SERVES 9

Wildly tender and moist, this cake makes perfect use of canned pumpkin. Save the leftover pumpkin for stirring into soups or stews.

Preheat the oven to 350°F (180°C). Grease an 8-inch square cake pan, and dust the pan with flour.

Whisk together the flour, baking powder, salt, cinnamon, cloves, and nutmeg in a small bowl.

Place the butter in a mixing bowl and, using an electric mixer, beat on medium-high speed until creamy. Gradually add the sugars, and beat until fluffy, about 4 minutes. Add the eggs one at a time, beating well after each addition. Reduce the speed to low, and add the flour mixture and the pumpkin a little at a time, beginning and ending with the flour mixture. Beat until just smooth. Add the vanilla, and beat 30 seconds. Fold in the toasted pecans. The batter will be thick. Scrape the batter into the prepared pan.

Bake the cake 30 to 35 minutes, until a tester inserted in the center comes out clean. Place the pan on a wire rack to cool.

To prepare the topping, combine the butter, cream, brown sugar, coconut, and vanilla in a saucepan, and heat over medium heat. Bring to a boil, and cook 2 minutes, stirring constantly. Let cool slightly, then pour over the warm cake in the pan.

cake

1¼ cups all-purpose flour (150g)

¾ teaspoon baking powder

½ teaspoon salt

¼ teaspoon ground cinnamon

¼ teaspoon ground cloves

¼ teaspoon ground nutmeg

6 tablespoons unsalted butter, softened (84g)

½ cup granulated sugar (99g)

½ cup packed light brown sugar (107g)

2 eggs, room temperature

¾ cup canned pure pumpkin (183g)

1 teaspoon vanilla extract

½ cup chopped pecans, toasted

topping

2 tablespoons unsalted butter

2 tablespoons heavy cream

3 tablespoons light brown sugar

⅓ cup unsweetened coconut flakes or shredded coconut

½ teaspoon vanilla extract

tiny tres leches cake

SERVES 9

*D*on't save this for Cinco de Mayo. It's a cinch to make, so any night can be a festival night. Make the cake and milk syrup an hour or two ahead of serving time, so that there's plenty of time for them to chill in the refrigerator.

Preheat the oven to 350°F (180°C). Grease an 8-inch square cake pan, and dust the pan with flour.

Whisk together the flour, baking powder, and salt in a small bowl.

Place the oil and sugar in a mixing bowl, and beat on medium-high speed about 2 minutes. Add the eggs one at a time, beating well after each addition. Reduce the speed to low, and add the flour mixture and the milk a little at a time, beginning and ending with the flour mixture. Add the vanilla, and beat 30 seconds. The batter will be thin. Pour the batter into the prepared pan.

Bake the cake 18 to 20 minutes, until the top springs back when lightly pressed and a tester inserted in the center comes out clean. Place the pan on a wire rack, and let the cake cool 15 minutes. Remove the cake from the pan, and return it, top side up, to the rack to cool completely.

To prepare the milk syrup, combine the evaporated milk, sweetened condensed milk, heavy cream, and rum in a small bowl. Whisk until well blended.

When the cake is cool, place it on a cake plate (one with a rim or sides works best). Spoon about two-thirds of the milk syrup over the top of the cake. Refrigerate the cake at least one hour. Refrigerate the remaining milk syrup.

To serve, spoon a bit of the remaining milk syrup onto a plate, and place a square of the cake on top. Top the cake with a dollop of Sweetened Whipped Cream.

cake

1¼ cups all-purpose flour (150g)

1 teaspoon baking powder

⅛ teaspoon salt

¼ cup canola oil (50g)

¾ cup sugar (150g)

4 eggs, room temperature

7 tablespoons whole milk (93g)

1 teaspoon vanilla extract

Sweetened Whipped Cream (page 151)

milk syrup

½ cup evaporated milk

½ cup sweetened condensed milk

⅔ cup heavy cream

2 tablespoons white or dark rum

carrot loaf

SERVES 9

This cake is equally good for breakfast as it is for an after-dinner treat. It's a dream served warm.

Preheat the oven to 350°F (180°C). Grease an 8½ by 4½-inch loaf pan. Line the pan with parchment paper, bringing the sides up over the long edges of the pan. Grease the parchment. Dust the pan with flour.

Whisk together 1 cup of the flour, baking powder, baking soda, salt, cinnamon, and nutmeg in a small bowl.

Toss the raisins and nuts with the remaining 1 tablespoon of flour in a small bowl.

Combine the sugars and eggs in a mixing bowl. Using an electric mixer at medium-high speed, beat for 2 minutes. Slowly add the oil while continuing to beat. Add the vanilla, and beat 30 seconds.

Fold in the flour mixture until blended. Fold in the carrots, raisins, and nuts. Scrape the batter into the prepared pan.

Bake the cake 45 to 50 minutes, until a tester inserted in the center comes out clean. Place the pan on a wire rack, and let the cake cool 10 minutes. Remove the cake from the pan, and return it, top side up, to the rack. Serve the cake warm or let it cool completely.

1 cup plus 1 tablespoon all-purpose flour (120g + 7g)

1 teaspoon baking powder

½ teaspoon baking soda

½ teaspoon salt

1 teaspoon ground cinnamon

¼ teaspoon ground nutmeg

⅓ cup golden raisins

⅓ cup chopped walnuts or pecans

½ cup granulated sugar (99g)

¼ cup packed brown sugar (53g)

2 eggs, room temperature

⅔ cup canola oil (131g)

1 teaspoon vanilla extract

1½ cups grated carrot (about 4 carrots, 170g)

butterscotch pecan loaf

SERVES 8

*S*uper buttery and oh, so delicious. No mixer is needed for this quick-as-a-wink loaf cake.

Preheat the oven to 350°F (180°C). Grease an 8½ by 4½-inch loaf pan. Dust the pan with flour.

Melt the butter in a small saucepan. Let cool slightly.

Whisk together the sugar and yogurt in a large bowl. Add the eggs, one at a time, whisking to blend well after each addition.

Whisk together the flour, baking powder, baking soda, and salt in a medium bowl. Add to the yogurt mixture in three additions, whisking after each addition until just combined. Fold in the butter a little at a time, using a rubber spatula. Fold in the chips and pecans. Scrape the batter into the prepared pan.

Bake the cake 45 to 50 minutes, until the cake is golden brown on top and a tester inserted in the center comes out clean. Place the pan on a wire rack, and let the cake cool 10 minutes. Remove the cake from the pan, and return it, top side up, to the rack to cool completely.

⅔ cup unsalted butter (146g)

1 cup sugar (198g)

⅔ cup plain yogurt, room temperature (160g)

3 eggs, room temperature

1¾ cups all-purpose flour (210g)

1½ teaspoons baking powder

¼ teaspoon baking soda

¼ teaspoon salt

½ cup butterscotch chips

½ cup chopped pecans, toasted

ricotta cake

SERVES 8

*S*imilar to a cheesecake, this little delight uses cornstarch instead of flour. Serve it with macerated strawberries or Raspberry Wine Coulis.

Preheat the oven to 350°F (180°C). Grease an 8-inch round cake pan.

Place the eggs, egg white, and sugar in a mixing bowl. Using the whisk attachment, beat on high speed until quadrupled in volume, about 5 minutes. Reduce the speed to medium, and add the ricotta cheese. Beat until smooth. Add the sour cream, cornstarch, baking powder, vanilla, oil, lemon peel, and salt. Beat until blended. The batter will be thin. Pour the batter into the prepared pan.

Bake the cake 45 to 50 minutes, until puffed and golden brown on top. Place the pan on a wire rack, and let the cake cool 20 minutes. Serve with macerated strawberries or Raspberry Wine Coulis.

2 eggs, room temperature

1 egg white, room temperature

6 tablespoons sugar (74g)

12 ounces whole-milk ricotta cheese, room temperature (340g)

3 ounces sour cream, room temperature (84g)

1½ tablespoons cornstarch

½ teaspoon baking powder

¾ teaspoon vanilla extract

2 teaspoons canola oil (8g)

½ teaspoon finely grated lemon peel

½ teaspoon salt

Strawberries, macerated (see sub-recipe on page 79) or Raspberry Wine Coulis (page 149)

tea cakes

MAKES 1½ TO 2 DOZEN

A Southern favorite, Tea Cakes are little cakey cookies that you can sprinkle with coarse sugar or frost with Easy Chocolate Buttercream Frosting. Despite their name, I like them with a glass of cold milk.

1¾ cups all-purpose flour (210g)

1 teaspoon baking powder

½ teaspoon baking soda

¼ teaspoon salt

¼ teaspoon ground nutmeg

½ cup unsalted butter, softened (113g)

¾ cup granulated sugar (150g)

1 egg, room temperature

3 tablespoons buttermilk, room temperature

½ teaspoon vanilla extract

Coarse sugar or Easy Chocolate Buttercream Frosting (page 148)

Whisk together the flour, baking powder, baking soda, salt, and nutmeg in a small bowl.

Place the butter in a mixing bowl, and using an electric mixer at medium-high speed, beat until creamy. Add the granulated sugar, and beat until fluffy, about 4 minutes. Add the egg, and beat until smooth. Reduce the speed to low, and add the flour mixture and buttermilk a little at a time, beginning and ending with the flour mixture and beating until just combined. Add the vanilla, and beat 30 seconds.

Place a large piece of plastic wrap on the work surface. Scrape the dough onto the plastic. Form the dough into a disk, and wrap securely. Place in the refrigerator at least 2 hours or up to overnight.

Preheat the oven to 325°F (165°C). Lightly grease 2 baking sheets. Dust flour over a cutting board or work surface. Working with half the dough at a time, roll the dough to a thickness of ⅓ inch. Using a biscuit cutter or straight-sided glass (about 2¾-inch diameter), cut the dough into rounds, and place them on the prepared baking sheets 1 inch apart. Bake the Tea Cakes for 9 to 10 minutes, until light golden. Remove from the oven, and sprinkle about ¼ teaspoon coarse sugar on top (omit if frosting). Let the Tea Cakes cool on the pan for 5 minutes, then using a spatula, transfer them to a wire rack to cool completely.

If frosting, spread the buttercream on top, leaving a ¼-inch unfrosted edge. To harden the frosting, refrigerate the Tea Cakes in a single layer for 20 minutes. Store frosted cakes in a cool place.

2

what a fruitcake

My mother, Gene Brimm Floyd, was a wonderful baker. Her biscuits, cornbread, and rolls were pure heaven, and yes, we had hot homemade bread every night with dinner. Her pies were masterpieces. Chocolate meringue was our favorite—and if you've never had leftover chocolate meringue pie for breakfast (with a side of oatmeal), well, more's the pity.

Her fruitcake, though, was tough for me to embrace. It was definitely moist and fruity and had enough whiskey in it to sink a sailor. But it was basically a brick—weighing in at a couple of pounds. Bless her heart, she made them every Christmas and gave them away by the dozens.

The fruitcakes here are not that of that ilk. They're lighter and brighter and put fresh fruits and berries in the starring role. Serve them for dessert or breakfast.

fresh apple cake

SERVES 9

The aroma of this cake coming from the oven is what a fall day at my grandmother's house smelled like. Be sure to use a tart baking apple, like Granny Smith or Cortland. Serve the cake with Lemon Butter Sauce and a scoop of vanilla ice cream.

5 tablespoons butter, softened (70g)

1 cup sugar (198g)

1 egg, room temperature

1 cup all-purpose flour (120g)

1 teaspoon baking soda

¼ teaspoon salt

½ teaspoon ground cinnamon

2 large tart apples, peeled, cored, and chopped

1 cup coarsely chopped walnuts

Lemon Butter Sauce (page 145)

Vanilla ice cream

Preheat the oven to 350°F (180°C). Grease a 9-inch square cake pan.

Place the butter in a mixing bowl, and beat with an electric mixer at medium-high speed until creamy. Add the sugar, and beat until fluffy, about 5 minutes. Add the egg, and beat until combined. Fold in the flour, baking soda, salt, cinnamon, apples, and walnuts. The batter will be thick, and it will look as though there is barely enough batter to coat the fruit and nuts. Spoon the batter into the prepared pan, and smooth the top.

Bake the cake 35 to 40 minutes. Remove the cake from oven, and let the cake cool slightly. Serve it warm with Lemon Butter Sauce and ice cream on top.

allspice applesauce cake

SERVES 9

This super moist cake is great for packing in lunches or for an afternoon snack.

Preheat the oven to 350°F (180°C). Grease an 8-inch square cake pan, and dust the pan with flour.

Combine the flour, baking soda, salt, allspice, and ginger in a small bowl.

Place the egg and sugars in a mixing bowl. Using an electric mixer, beat at medium speed until light, about 3 minutes. Add the applesauce, oil, and vanilla, and beat until blended. Reduce the speed to low, and add the flour mixture a little at a time, beating until just smooth. Fold in the pecans. Scrape the batter into the prepared pan.

Bake the cake 20 to 25 minutes, until a tester inserted in the center comes out clean. Place the pan on a wire rack, and sprinkle with the coarse sugar while still warm. Let the cake cool completely.

1 cup all-purpose flour (120g)

¾ teaspoon baking soda

½ teaspoon salt

1 teaspoon allspice

¼ teaspoon ground ginger

1 egg, room temperature

½ cup granulated sugar (99g)

¼ cup packed light brown sugar (50g)

¾ cup unsweetened applesauce (183g)

⅓ cup canola oil (65g)

½ teaspoon vanilla extract

¼ cup chopped pecans, toasted

Coarse sugar, optional

blueberry pecan cake

SERVES 9

*T*he pecan topping makes this cake rich and toasty all on its own, but to gild the lily, serve it slightly warm with vanilla ice cream. Leftovers are great for breakfast.

Preheat the oven to 350°F (180°C). Grease an 8-inch round cake pan. Line the pan with parchment paper, and grease the parchment. Dust the pan with flour.

To prepare the topping, place the pecans, melted butter, flour, brown sugar, and salt in a small bowl. Stir with a fork until well mixed.

To prepare the cake, combine 1¼ cups of the flour, baking powder, baking soda, and salt in a small bowl.

Toss the blueberries with the remaining 1 tablespoon of flour in a small bowl.

Place the butter in a mixing bowl. Using an electric mixer, beat at medium-high speed until creamy. Add the granulated sugar, and beat until fluffy, about 5 minutes. Add the eggs and egg yolk, one at a time, and beat until combined. Add the vanilla and lemon peel, and beat until combined. Reduce the speed to low, and add the flour mixture and sour cream a little at a time, beginning and ending with the flour mixture. Beat until just combined.

Spoon half of the batter into the prepared pan, and smooth the top with an offset spatula. Scatter the blueberries on top. Spoon the remaining batter on top, and smooth with the spatula.

Crumble the topping evenly over the batter.

Bake the cake 30 to 35 minutes, until it begins to pull away from the sides of the pan and a tester inserted in the center comes out clean. Place the pan on a wire rack, and let the cake cool 10 minutes. Remove the cake from the pan, and return it, top side up, to the rack to cool completely.

topping

½ cup pecans, chopped

¼ cup butter, melted

⅓ cup all-purpose flour

⅓ cup light brown sugar

¼ teaspoon salt

cake

1¼ cups plus 1 tablespoon all-purpose flour (150g + 7g)

1 teaspoon baking powder

¼ teaspoon baking soda

½ teaspoon salt

¾ cup fresh blueberries

7 tablespoons unsalted butter, softened (98g)

1 cup granulated sugar (198g)

2 eggs, room temperature

1 egg yolk, room temperature

1 teaspoon vanilla extract

1 teaspoon finely grated lemon peel

7 tablespoons sour cream (106g)

cherry-almond clafouti

SERVES 6

Kind of like a crustless pie, this little dessert is a perfect blend of slightly sweet, custardy cake and tart cherries.

. . . .

Preheat the oven to 400°F (200°C). Grease an 8-inch cast-iron skillet or casserole dish. Dust with 1 tablespoon of the granulated sugar. Spread the cherries in the bottom of the pan.

Combine the flour, the remaining granulated sugar, and salt in a large bowl. Whisk in the eggs and butter until smooth. Add the milk, heavy cream, vanilla, and ground almonds. Whisk until well blended. Pour the batter over the cherries.

Bake the clafouti 18 to 20 minutes, until the edges are puffed and brown and the center is just set. Place the pan on a wire rack, and let the clafouti cool 10 minutes. Dust with confectioner's sugar. Cut the clafouti into wedges to serve. Top with a dollop of slightly Sweetened Whipped Cream if desired.

½ cup granulated sugar, divided (99g)

1¾ to 2 cups tart cherries, pitted

5½ tablespoons all-purpose flour (42g)

¼ teaspoon salt

3 eggs, room temperature, slightly beaten

1½ tablespoons butter, melted and cooled (21g)

½ cup whole milk (114g)

⅓ cup heavy cream (79g)

½ teaspoon vanilla extract

2 tablespoons finely ground almonds

Confectioner's sugar

Sweetened Whipped Cream (page 151), optional

citrus cake

SERVES 8

A perfect little treat for winter months, when citrus is at its peak, this cake is sweet and tart at the same time.

Preheat the oven to 325°F (165°C). Grease an 8-inch round cake pan. Line with parchment paper. Grease the parchment. Dust the pan with flour.

Whisk together the flour, baking soda, and salt in a medium bowl.

Combine the buttermilk, orange juice, and lemon juice in a small bowl.

Place the butter in a mixing bowl, and using an electric mixer at medium-high speed, beat until creamy. Add the granulated sugar, and beat until fluffy, about 5 minutes. Add the egg and egg yolk one at a time, beating until smooth. Reduce the speed to low, and add the flour mixture and buttermilk mixture a little at a time, beginning and ending with flour mixture, beating until just combined. Add the orange and lemon peel, and beat 30 seconds. Pour the batter into the prepared pan.

Bake the cake 25 to 30 minutes, until the top is golden brown and a tester inserted in the center comes out clean. Place the pan on a wire rack, and let the cake cool 10 minutes. Remove the cake from the pan, and return it, top side up, to the rack to cool about 15 minutes.

To prepare the frosting, place the butter in a mixing bowl, and using an electric mixer at medium speed, beat until creamy. Reduce the speed to low, and gradually spoon in the confectioner's sugar. Beat until smooth. Add the salt and the orange and lemon peel and juice. Increase the speed to medium-high, and beat until the frosting reaches the desired consistency. Spread the frosting on top of the slightly warm cake, letting the frosting drip down the sides of the cake. Sprinkle the additional orange peel on top of the cake.

cake

- 1½ cups all-purpose flour (180g)
- ¼ teaspoon baking soda
- ¼ teaspoon salt
- ¼ cup buttermilk (56g)
- 2 tablespoons fresh orange juice
- 1 tablespoon fresh lemon juice
- 6 tablespoons unsalted butter, softened (84g)
- 1 cup granulated sugar (198g)
- 1 egg, room temperature
- 1 egg yolk, room temperature
- 1 teaspoon finely grated orange peel
- 2 teaspoons finely grated lemon peel

buttery citrus frosting

- 2 tablespoons unsalted butter, softened (28g)
- 1 cup confectioner's sugar (114g)
- ¼ teaspoon salt
- 1 teaspoon finely grated orange peel, plus more for sprinkling on top
- 2 teaspoons finely grated lemon peel
- 1 tablespoon fresh orange juice
- 1 tablespoon fresh lemon juice

fig and orange cake

SERVES 9

ake sure your dried figs are fresh and moist. The glaze adds sweetness and an extra kick of citrus flavor.

Preheat the oven to 350°F (180°C). Grease an 8-inch square cake pan. Line with parchment paper. Grease the parchment. Dust the pan with flour.

Remove the hard stems from the figs, and chop the figs coarsely (6 to 8 pieces per fig). Place them in a bowl, and cover them with boiling water. Let them soak 10 minutes. Drain off the liquid.

Whisk together the flour, granulated sugar, baking powder, and salt in a large bowl.

Whisk together the oil, milk, and eggs in a small bowl. Pour the milk mixture into the flour mixture, and fold together with a rubber spatula until just combined. Fold in the drained figs, orange peel, and vanilla. Scrape the batter into the prepared pan.

Bake the cake 23 to 25 minutes, until a tester inserted in the center comes out clean. Place the pan on a wire rack, and let the cake cool completely.

To prepare the glaze, whisk together the confectioner's sugar, orange juice, orange peel, and butter until smooth. Drizzle the glaze over the top of the cake. Cut the cake into squares, and serve from the pan.

cake

7 ounces dried figs (198g)

Boiling water

1½ cups all-purpose flour (180g)

1 cup granulated sugar (198g)

1 teaspoon baking powder

½ teaspoon salt

½ cup olive oil (99g)

½ cup whole milk, room temperature (114g)

2 eggs, room temperature

2 teaspoons finely grated orange peel

1 teaspoon vanilla extract

glaze

½ cup confectioner's sugar (57g)

2 tablespoons fresh orange juice

¼ teaspoon finely grated orange peel

1 tablespoon unsalted butter, melted

lemon-rosemary yogurt loaf

SERVES 8

Fresh rosemary adds a heady aroma to this loaf cake. If you don't like rosemary, substitute fresh thyme. Serve slices of this cake with lemon sorbet and raspberries.

Preheat the oven to 350°F (180°C). Grease an 8¼ by 4½-inch loaf pan. Dust the pan with flour.

Combine the flour, baking powder, baking soda, and salt in a medium bowl.

Combine the yogurt, vanilla, and lemon juice in a glass measuring cup.

Place the butter in a mixing bowl. Using an electric mixer, beat at medium-high speed until creamy. Add the sugar, and beat until fluffy, about 4 minutes. Add the eggs and egg yolk one at a time, beating well after each addition. Reduce the speed to low, and add the flour mixture and the yogurt mixture a little at a time, beginning and ending with the flour mixture. Beat until just blended. Add the lemon peel and rosemary, and beat 30 seconds. Scrape the batter into the prepared pan.

Bake the cake 40 to 45 minutes, until lightly browned and a tester inserted in the center comes out clean. Place the pan on a wire rack, and let the cake cool 10 minutes.

To prepare the syrup, combine the sugar and lemon juice in a small saucepan, and heat over medium heat until the sugar is dissolved.

Remove the cake from the pan, and return it, top side up, to the rack set over a baking sheet to catch drips. Pour the warm syrup over the warm cake. Let the cake cool completely.

cake

1½ cups all-purpose flour (180g)

¼ teaspoon baking powder

¼ teaspoon baking soda

½ teaspoon salt

6 tablespoons plain yogurt, room temperature (90g)

½ teaspoon vanilla extract

2 tablespoons fresh lemon juice

6 tablespoons unsalted butter, softened (84g)

1 cup sugar (198g)

2 eggs, room temperature

1 egg yolk, room temperature

Finely grated peel of 1 lemon

1 teaspoon finely chopped fresh rosemary

lemon syrup

2 tablespoons sugar

2 tablespoons fresh lemon juice

lemon cornmeal cake

SERVES 8

No mixer is required for this delicately tart cake that gets its pleasant grainy texture from cornmeal. To set it off perfectly, pile fresh blueberries on top.

Preheat the oven to 350°F (180°C). Grease an 8-inch round cake pan. Line the pan with parchment paper. Grease the parchment. Dust the pan with flour.

Whisk together the sour cream, granulated sugar, and eggs in a large bowl. Add the flour, cornmeal, baking powder, baking soda, salt, and lemon peel, and whisk until smooth. Stir in the vanilla, canola oil, and lemon juice. Scrape the batter into the prepared pan.

Bake the cake 25 to 30 minutes, until a tester inserted in the center comes out clean. Place the pan on a wire rack, and let the cake cool 10 minutes. Cut the cake into wedges to serve.

To prepare the glaze, combine the lemon juice and confectioner's sugar in a small bowl, and whisk until smooth. Using a pastry brush, spread the glaze over the warm cake.

cake

½ cup sour cream (120g)

1 cup granulated sugar (198g)

3 eggs, room temperature

1¼ cups all-purpose flour (150g)

½ cup white medium-ground cornmeal (45g)

1¼ teaspoons baking powder

¼ teaspoon baking soda

½ teaspoon salt

Finely grated peel of 1 lemon

½ teaspoon vanilla extract

½ cup canola oil (99g)

1 tablespoon fresh lemon juice

glaze

2 tablespoons lemon juice

6 tablespoons confectioner's sugar

lemon-sour cream pound loaf

SERVES 8

*S*erve slices of this loaf with macerated berries and Sweetened Whipped Cream.

Preheat the oven to 350°F (180°C). Grease an 8½ by 4½-inch loaf pan. Dust the pan with flour.

Whisk together the flour, baking powder, baking soda, and salt in a small bowl.

Place the butter in a mixing bowl, and using an electric mixer at medium-high speed, beat until creamy. Add the sugars, and beat until fluffy, about 5 minutes. Add the eggs one at a time, beating well after each addition. Reduce the speed to low, and add the flour mixture and the sour cream a little at a time, beginning and ending with the flour mixture. Add the vanilla, lemon juice, and lemon peel, and beat 30 seconds. Scrape the batter into the prepared pan.

Bake the cake 30 to 35 minutes, until a tester inserted in the center comes out clean. Place the pan on a wire rack, and let the cake cool 15 minutes. Remove the cake from the pan, and return it, top side up, to the rack to cool completely.

To prepare the berries, place the fruit, sugar, and orange juice in a bowl. Let stand at room temperature until the fruit begins to release its juices, about 30 minutes. If desired, mash some of the fruit against the side of the bowl before spooning it onto slices of the cake. Top with Sweetened Whipped Cream (page 151) if desired.

cake

1 cup all-purpose flour (120g)

½ teaspoon baking powder

⅓ teaspoon baking soda

¼ teaspoon salt

5 tablespoons unsalted butter, softened (70g)

½ cup packed light brown sugar (106g)

2 tablespoons granulated sugar (24g)

2 eggs, room temperature

½ cup sour cream, room temperature (120g)

½ teaspoon vanilla extract

2 tablespoons fresh lemon juice

1 teaspoon finely grated lemon peel

macerated berries

2 cups strawberries or blackberries

2 tablespoons granulated sugar

1 tablespoon orange juice

lime cake

SERVES 9

This tart little cake pairs beautifully with Lime Cream Cheese Frosting.

Preheat the oven to 350°F (180°C). Grease an 8-inch square cake pan. Dust the pan with flour.

Whisk together the flour, baking powder, and salt in a small bowl.

Place the butter in a mixing bowl, and using an electric mixer at medium-high speed, beat until creamy. Add the sugar, and beat until fluffy, about 5 minutes. Add the egg and egg yolk one at a time, beating well after each addition. Reduce the speed to low, and add the flour mixture and the milk a little at a time, beginning and ending with the flour mixture. Add half of the lime peel and the lime juice, and beat 30 seconds. Scrape the batter into the prepared pan.

Bake the cake 25 to 30 minutes, until a tester inserted in the center comes out clean. Place the pan on a wire rack, and let the cake cool 15 minutes. Remove the cake from the pan, and return it, top side up, to the rack to cool completely.

Frost the top of the cake with Lime Cream Cheese Frosting. Sprinkle the remaining lime peel on top.

1½ cups all-purpose flour (150g)

1½ teaspoons baking powder

½ teaspoon salt

¼ cup unsalted butter, softened (56g)

1 cup sugar (198g)

1 egg, room temperature

1 egg yolk, room temperature

10 tablespoons whole milk, room temperature (140g)

Finely grated peel of 2 limes, divided

1 tablespoon fresh lime juice

Lime Cream Cheese Frosting (page 144)

orange-pecan pound loaf

SERVES 8

*I*f you have any leftovers, slice and toast them, then spread with a little warm butter for breakfast.

Preheat the oven to 350°F (180°C). Grease an 8½ by 4½-inch loaf pan. Line with parchment paper, bringing the paper up and over the long sides of the pan. Grease the parchment. Dust the pan with flour.

Whisk together the flour, baking powder, baking soda, and salt in a medium bowl.

Combine the buttermilk, orange juice, and vanilla in a small bowl.

Place the butter in a mixing bowl, and using an electric mixer at medium-high speed, beat until creamy. Add the sugar, and beat until fluffy, about 5 minutes. Add the eggs one at a time, beating after each addition until smooth. Add the orange peel. Reduce the speed to low, and add the flour mixture and the buttermilk mixture a little at a time, beginning and ending with the flour mixture. Beat until just blended. Fold in the pecans. Scrape the batter into the prepared pan.

Bake the cake 40 to 45 minutes, until the cake is golden brown on the top and a tester inserted in the center comes out clean. Place the pan on a wire rack, and let the cake cool 10 minutes.

To make the syrup, combine the sugar and orange juice in a small saucepan. Cook over medium heat until the sugar is dissolved.

Remove the cake from the pan, and return it, top side up, to the rack set over a baking sheet. Brush the syrup over the top and sides of the cake while it is still warm. Let the cake cool completely.

cake

1½ cups all-purpose flour (180g)

¼ teaspoon baking powder

¼ teaspoon baking soda

½ teaspoon salt

6 tablespoons buttermilk, room temperature (84g)

¼ cup fresh orange juice (62g)

½ teaspoon vanilla extract

½ cup unsalted butter, softened (112g)

1 cup sugar (198g)

2 eggs, room temperature

2 tablespoons finely grated orange peel (about 2 oranges)

¼ cup chopped pecans

syrup

¼ cup sugar

¼ cup fresh orange juice

prune cake

SERVES 9

This old recipe is just as good today as it was when your grandmother made it. It's super moist with a sticky sweet topping that sinks in as you pour it over the warm cake.

. . . .

Preheat the oven to 300°F (150°C). Grease an 8-inch square cake pan, and dust with flour.

Place the prunes in a small saucepan, and cover with water. Bring to a boil over medium-high heat. Reduce the heat to low, and simmer 8 minutes. Remove from the heat, and drain off the liquid. Place the prunes on a plate, and mash with a fork.

Whisk together the flour, baking soda, salt, cinnamon, allspice, and nutmeg in a small bowl.

Combine the sugar and oil in a mixing bowl, and using an electric mixer at medium speed, beat 4 minutes. Add the eggs one at a time, beating well after each addition. Reduce the speed to low, and add the flour mixture and buttermilk a little at a time, beginning and ending with the flour mixture. Beat until just blended. The batter will be thin. Stir in the vanilla and prunes. Do not overmix. Pour the batter into the prepared pan.

Bake the cake 35 to 40 minutes, until a tester inserted in the center comes out clean. Place the pan on a wire rack, and let the cake cool.

During the last 10 minutes of baking time, prepare the topping. Combine the sugar, buttermilk, baking soda, and corn syrup in a small saucepan. Bring to a boil over medium-high heat. Cook, stirring constantly, 6 to 7 minutes, until the topping begins to brown and thicken. Remove from the heat, and stir in the vanilla. While the cake is still warm, pour the topping over the top of the cake, and spread with the back of a spoon.

cake

⅔ cup prunes (15 prunes, 136g)

1¼ cups all-purpose flour (150g)

1 teaspoon baking soda

½ teaspoon salt

½ teaspoon ground cinnamon

½ teaspoon allspice

½ teaspoon ground nutmeg

1 cup sugar (198g)

⅔ cup canola oil (131g)

2 eggs, room temperature

½ cup buttermilk, room temperature (148g)

½ teaspoon vanilla extract

topping

½ cup sugar

¼ cup buttermilk

¼ teaspoon baking soda

2 teaspoon light corn syrup

½ teaspoon vanilla extract

>3<
shrinking act

· · · · · · · · · ·

Full-blown glories are taken down a notch to family size proportions. Some of these cakes are made in single layers (8- or 9-inch cake pans), but others are geared toward two 6-inch layers. They're cute little beauties that will delight birthday girls and boys or a small gathering of friends. If your layers form a domed top during baking, you can level one or both layers by cutting off the top of the domed portion with a serrated knife. The 6-inch layers are a bit more difficult to frost than standard 8- or 9-inch layers, as they aren't as stable or firmly planted on the plate. One easy trick is to first frost the top of the bottom layer, and place the second layer on top. Then stick three or four long wooden skewers through the two layers. Frost the sides of the cake, remove the skewers, and frost the top.

· · · · · · · · · ·

chocolate malt cake

SERVES 8

Take a trip to the soda shop of your childhood for a tricked-up malted milkshake made into a cake.

Preheat the oven to 325°F (165°C). Grease two 6-inch round cake pans. Line the pans with parchment paper. Grease the parchment. Dust the pans with cocoa.

Combine the malted milk powder, flour, cocoa, baking soda, and salt in a medium bowl.

In a large bowl, whisk together the eggs, granulated sugar, oil, and vanilla. Add the flour mixture and milk a little at a time, beginning and ending with the flour mixture. Stir until just blended. Scrape the batter into the prepared pans.

Bake the cakes 30 to 35 minutes, until a tester inserted in the center comes out clean. Place the pans on a wire rack, and let the cakes cool 10 minutes. Remove the cakes from the pans, and return them, top side up, to the rack to cool completely.

Place the chocolate malt balls in a ziptop plastic bag. Seal the bag. Crush the malt balls using a meat mallet. If desired, place in a wire mesh sieve to sift out excess malt powder.

To prepare the frosting, combine the butter, vanilla, and malted milk powder in a mixing bowl. Beat with an electric mixer at medium-high speed until smooth. Add the melted chocolate and salt, and beat until smooth. Gradually add the confectioner's sugar and heavy cream, beating until smooth and spreadable.

Place one cake layer on a cake plate or stand. Spread about one-third of the frosting on top. Sprinkle with the crushed malt balls. Place the second cake layer on top. Spread the remaining frosting on the top and sides of the cake.

cake

1 cup plus 2 tablespoons malted milk powder (157g)

1 cup less 1 tablespoon all-purpose flour (113g)

6 tablespoons unsweetened cocoa powder (45g)

½ teaspoon baking soda

½ teaspoon salt

2 eggs, room temperature

¾ cup granulated sugar (149g)

6 tablespoons canola oil (74g)

1 teaspoon vanilla extract

¾ cup whole milk, room temperature (170g)

8 to 10 chocolate-covered malt balls, such as Whoppers

chocolate malt frosting & topping

½ cup unsalted butter, softened

1 teaspoon vanilla extract

½ cup malted milk powder

¼ cup bittersweet chocolate chips, melted and cooled lightly

¼ teaspoon salt

2 cups confectioner's sugar

2 tablespoons heavy cream

flourless chocolate cake

SERVES 6

Most flourless chocolate cake recipes are made in an 8- or 9-inch cake pan, or even a springform pan, and include a small amount of flour. This recipe is for a single 6-inch round cake pan and doesn't have a speck of flour. Serve it slightly warm with vanilla ice cream or Sweetened Whipped Cream (page 151).

4 ounces bittersweet chocolate, chopped (113g)

3 tablespoons butter (42g)

3 eggs, separated, room temperature

¼ cup granulated sugar (50g)

¼ teaspoon salt

Confectioner's sugar

Preheat the oven to 300°F (150°C). Grease a 6-inch round cake pan. Line the pan with parchment paper. Grease the parchment. Dust the pan with cocoa.

Melt the butter and chocolate in a glass measuring cup in the microwave, heating in 30 second increments and stirring until the chocolate melts completely. Let cool slightly.

Whisk the egg yolks in a small bowl. Add the chocolate mixture, and whisk until blended.

Place the egg whites in a medium bowl. Using a handheld mixer, beat the whites until soft peaks form. Sprinkle in the granulated sugar a little at a time, and continue beating until stiff peaks form. Scoop about one-third of the whites into the chocolate mixture to lighten the chocolate. Whisk until blended. Pour the chocolate mixture into the remaining whites, and gently fold until blended. Fold in the salt. Scrape the batter into the prepared pan, filling it to within ½ inch of the top. You may have a little batter left over.

Bake the cake 22 to 25 minutes, until a tester inserted in the center comes out almost clean. The cake will rise above the edge of the pan while baking and fall dramatically as it cools. Place the pan on a wire rack, and let the cake cool 10 minutes. Remove the cake from the pan, and place it, top side up, on a cake plate. Let it cool 10 minutes, then sprinkle the top with confectioner's sugar.

siren's chocolate cake

SERVES 8

*P*erfect for birthday celebrations, this luscious cake is made in two 6-inch round pans and frosted with Chocolate Ganache. To take matters over the top, spoon a bit of Raspberry Wine Coulis alongside each serving.

Preheat the oven to 350°F (150°C). Grease two 6-inch round cake pans. Line the pans with parchment. Grease the parchment. Dust the pans with cocoa powder.

Whisk together the flour, baking soda, and salt in a small bowl.

Melt the butter and chocolate in a double boiler over barely simmering water.

Combine the egg and buttermilk in a mixing bowl. Using an electric mixer, beat at medium speed until blended. Add the sugar and vanilla. Beat until blended. Reduce the speed to low, and add the flour mixture, beating until just blended. Pour in the chocolate mixture, and beat until blended. Pour the batter into the prepared pans.

Bake the cakes 25 to 28 minutes, until a tester inserted in the center comes out clean. Run a small knife around the inside of the pans. Place the pans on a wire rack, and let the cakes cool 10 minutes. Remove the cakes from the pans, and return them, top side up, to the rack to cool completely.

Place one layer on a cake plate. Frost with Chocolate Ganache. Place the second layer on top and frost top and sides of the cake.

1¼ cups all-purpose flour (150g)

1 teaspoon baking soda

¼ teaspoon salt

¼ cup unsalted butter (56g)

2 ounces unsweetened chocolate (57g)

1 egg

¾ cup buttermilk (169g)

1 cup sugar (198g)

1 teaspoon vanilla extract

Chocolate Ganache (page 150)

Raspberry Wine Coulis (page 149), optional

mexican chocolate cake

SERVES 8

Fill and frost this beauty with Chocolate Ganache, using the Mexican variation. Typical of Mexican chocolate, the spices—cinnamon and cayenne pepper—add pizzazz to this rich, moist cake.

Preheat the oven to 325°F (165°C). Grease two 6-inch round cake pans. Line the pans with parchment paper. Grease the parchment. Dust the pans with flour.

Whisk together the flour, cocoa, baking soda, salt, cinnamon, and cayenne in a medium bowl.

Combine the water, milk, and vanilla in a small bowl.

Place the butter in a mixing bowl. Using an electric mixer at medium-high speed, beat until creamy. Add the sugars, and beat until fluffy, about 5 minutes. Add the eggs one at a time, beating well after each addition. Reduce the speed to low, and add the flour mixture and milk mixture a little at a time, beginning and ending with the flour mixture. Beat until just smooth. Scrape the batter into the prepared pans and smooth the tops.

Bake the cakes 30 to 35 minutes, until a tester inserted into the center of the cakes comes out almost clean. Place the pans on a wire rack, and let the cakes cool 10 minutes. Remove the cakes from the pan, and return them, top side up, to the rack to cool completely.

Place one layer on a cake stand or plate. Spread about one-third of the ganache on top. Place the second layer on top, and spread the remaining ganache over the top and sides of the cake.

1¼ cups all-purpose flour (150g)

7 tablespoons unsweetened cocoa (53g)

1 teaspoon baking soda

½ teaspoon salt

½ teaspoon ground cinnamon

⅛ teaspoon cayenne pepper

⅔ cup water (156g)

¼ cup whole milk, room temperature (56g)

1 teaspoon vanilla extract

6 tablespoons unsalted butter, softened (84g)

½ cup packed brown sugar (106g)

½ cup granulated sugar (99g)

2 eggs, room temperature

Chocolate Ganache, Mexican variation (page 150)

hummingbird cake

SERVES 8

*S*uper moist with a tropical flavor from the banana and pineapple, Hummingbird Cake is perfect for special occasions. No mixer required! Save 1 tablespoon of the pineapple juice drained from the can to add to the Cream Cheese Frosting.

Preheat the oven to 325°F (165°C). Grease two 6-inch round cake pans. Line the pans with parchment paper. Grease the parchment. Dust the pans with flour.

Whisk together the flour, sugar, baking soda, salt, and cinnamon in a large bowl. Add the eggs, oil, and vanilla, and stir until combined. Stir in the pineapple, banana, and pecans. Scrape the batter into the prepared pans.

Bake the cakes 30 to 35 minutes, until a tester inserted in the center of the cakes comes out clean. Place the pans on a wire rack, and let the cakes cool 10 minutes. Remove the cakes from the pans, and return them, top side up, to the rack to cakes cool completely.

Place one layer on a cake stand or plate. Frost the top with about one-third of the Cream Cheese Frosting. Place the second layer on top, and frost the top of it. Decorate the top with toasted pecans.

1½ cups all-purpose flour (180g)

1 cup sugar (198g)

½ teaspoon baking soda

½ teaspoon salt

½ teaspoon ground cinnamon

2 eggs, slightly beaten, room temperature

½ cup canola oil (99g)

½ teaspoon vanilla extract

4 ounces canned crushed pineapple, drained (114g)

1 tablespoon pineapple juice reserved from can

1 large ripe banana, mashed

½ cup chopped pecans

Cream Cheese Frosting (page 144)

Toasted whole and chopped pecans

maple cake

with MAPLE FROSTING

SERVES 8

This fall beauty benefits from a darker, intensely flavored maple syrup, labeled grade B in the grocery store. If you can't find it, any pure maple syrup will work.

Preheat the oven to 325°F (165°C). Grease two 6-inch round cake pans. Line the pans with parchment paper. Grease the parchment. Dust the pans with flour.

Whisk together the flour, baking powder, baking soda, and salt in a medium bowl.

Place the butter in a mixing bowl. Using an electric mixer at medium-high speed, beat until creamy. Add the granulated sugar and maple syrup, and beat until fluffy, about 5 minutes. Add the egg and egg yolk one at a time, beating well after each addition. Reduce the speed to low, and add the flour mixture and yogurt a little at a time, beginning and ending with the flour mixture. Beat until just smooth. Add the vanilla, and beat 30 seconds. The batter will be thick. Scrape the batter into the prepared pans, and smooth the tops.

Bake the cakes 25 to 30 minutes, until a tester inserted in the center comes out almost clean. Place the pans on a wire rack, and let the cakes cool 10 minutes. Remove the cakes from the pans, and return them, top side up, to the rack to cool completely.

To prepare the frosting, combine the maple syrup and melted butter in a bowl. Whisk until well blended. Whisk in the confectioner's sugar, a little at a time. Stir in the vanilla and salt.

Place one layer on a cake stand or plate. Spread about one-third of the frosting on top. Place the second layer on top, and frost the top of the cake. Decorate the top with toasted walnuts.

cake

1⅔ cups all-purpose flour (200g)

1½ teaspoons baking powder

¼ teaspoon baking soda

¼ teaspoon salt

¾ cup unsalted butter, softened (168g)

6 tablespoons granulated sugar (74g)

½ cup pure maple syrup

1 egg, room temperature

1 egg yolk, room temperature

½ cup plain whole-milk yogurt, room temperature

¾ teaspoon vanilla extract

maple frosting

⅓ cup pure maple syrup

3 tablespoons unsalted butter, melted

2½ cups confectioner's sugar

¼ teaspoon vanilla extract

½ teaspoon salt

¼ cup chopped walnuts, toasted

mocha cake

SERVES 8

*C*offee and chocolate in a sweet little layer cake—perfect for birthday celebrations.

Preheat the oven to 350°F (180°C). Grease two 6-inch round cake pans. Line the pans with parchment paper. Grease the parchment. Dust the pans with cocoa powder.

Place the chocolate in a glass measuring cup. Microwave in 30-second increments, stirring after each, until melted and smooth. Stir in the espresso powder.

Whisk together the flour, baking soda, and salt in a small bowl.

Place the butter in a mixing bowl, and using an electric mixer at medium-high speed, beat until creamy. Add the brown sugar, and beat until fluffy, about 4 minutes. Add the eggs and egg yolk one at a time, beating well after each addition. Add the chocolate mixture, and beat until well blended. Reduce the speed to low, and add the flour and buttermilk a little at a time, beginning and ending with the flour mixture. Add the vanilla, and beat 30 seconds. Scrape the batter into the prepared pans.

Bake the cakes 25 to 30 minutes, until a tester inserted in the center comes out clean. Place the pans on a wire rack, and let the cakes cool 10 minutes. Remove the cakes from the pans, and return them, top side up, to the rack to cool completely.

To prepare the buttercream, place the chocolate in a glass measuring cup. Microwave in 30-second increments, stirring after each, until melted and smooth. Stir in the espresso powder.

Place the butter in a mixing bowl. Using an electric mixer at medium speed, beat until creamy. Add the chocolate mixture and salt, and beat until smooth. Gradually add the confectioner's sugar, beating until completely smooth. Add the vanilla, and beat 30 seconds.

Place one cake layer on a cake plate or stand. Spread about one-third of the buttercream on top. Place the second layer on top. Frost the top and sides of the cake with the remaining buttercream.

cake

2½ ounces dark chocolate, chopped

1 tablespoon plus 1 teaspoon instant espresso powder

1¼ cups all-purpose flour (150g)

¾ teaspoon baking soda

½ teaspoon salt

⅔ cup unsalted butter, softened (149g)

1 cup packed light brown sugar (213g)

2 eggs, room temperature

1 egg yolk, room temperature

⅔ cup buttermilk, room temperature (149g)

¾ teaspoon vanilla extract

mocha buttercream frosting

2 ounces dark chocolate

1 teaspoon instant espresso powder

4 teaspoons whole milk

½ cup unsalted butter, softened

⅛ teaspoon salt

2 cups confectioner's sugar

½ teaspoon vanilla extract

spice cake

with BROWN SUGAR BUTTERCREAM FROSTING

SERVES 9

With its heady dose of cinnamon, ginger, cloves, and nutmeg, this tender cake screams fall. The brown sugar adds a tiny crunch to the creamy frosting.

Preheat the oven to 325°F (165°C). Grease two 6-inch round cake pans. Line the pans with parchment paper. Grease the parchment. Dust the pans with flour.

Whisk together the flour, baking powder, baking soda, salt, ginger, cinnamon, cloves, and nutmeg in a small bowl.

Place the butter in a mixing bowl. Using an electric mixer at medium-high speed, beat until creamy. Add the brown sugar, and beat until fluffy, about 5 minutes. Add the eggs and egg yolk one at a time, beating well after each addition. Reduce the speed to low, and add the flour mixture and buttermilk a little at a time, beginning and ending with the flour mixture. Beat until just smooth. Add the vanilla, and beat 30 seconds. Scrape the batter into the prepared pans.

Bake the cakes 25 to 30 minutes, until a tester inserted in the center comes out almost clean. Place the pans on a wire rack, and let the cakes cool 10 minutes. Remove the cakes from the pans, and return them, top side up, to the rack to cool completely.

To prepare the frosting, place the butter and brown sugar in a mixing bowl. Using an electric mixer at medium speed, beat until smooth, about 3 minutes. Add the confectioner's sugar a little at a time, beating until smooth. Add the salt, vanilla, and milk, beating until smooth. Add more milk as needed to reach spreading consistency.

Place one cake layer on a plate or cake stand, and top with about one-third of the frosting. Place the second cake layer on top. Frost the top and sides of the cake.

cake

1⅓ cups all-purpose flour (160g)

1¼ teaspoons baking powder

½ teaspoon baking soda

½ teaspoon salt

½ teaspoon ground ginger

½ teaspoon ground cinnamon

¼ teaspoon ground cloves

¼ teaspoon ground nutmeg

½ cup unsalted butter, softened (113g)

1 cup packed brown sugar (213g)

2 eggs, room temperature

1 egg yolk, room temperature

⅔ cup buttermilk, room temperature (139g)

½ teaspoon vanilla extract

brown sugar buttercream

½ cup unsalted butter, softened

¼ cup packed brown sugar

1½ cups confectioner's sugar, sifted

¼ teaspoon salt

½ teaspoon vanilla extract

1 tablespoon whole milk (or more)

strawberry cake

SERVES 8

Use fresh or frozen strawberries in this moist cake. For frozen strawberries, let them thaw completely in a colander, and drain off the juice. Make a double batch of the Cream Cheese Frosting to ice the top and sides of this layered treat.

Preheat the oven to 350°F (180°C). Grease two 6-inch round cake pans. Line the pans with parchment paper. Grease the parchment. Dust the pans with flour.

Combine 1½ cups strawberries (210g) and the water in a small saucepan. Bring to a boil over medium-high heat, and boil 5 minutes, until beginning to thicken. Let cool 15 minutes.

Whisk together the flour, cornstarch, baking powder, and salt in a medium bowl.

Place the butter in a mixing bowl, and using an electric mixer at medium-high speed, beat until creamy. Add the sugar and beat until fluffy, about 5 minutes. Add the egg whites one at a time, and beat until well combined. Reduce the speed to low, and add the flour mixture and milk a little at a time, beginning and ending with the flour mixture. Beat until just smooth. Add the vanilla, and beat 30 seconds. Fold in the cooked strawberries and the ¼ cup sliced strawberries. The batter will be thin. Scrape into the prepared pans.

Bake the cakes 35 to 40 minutes, until a tester inserted into the center comes out almost clean. Place the pans on a wire rack, and let the cakes cool 10 minutes. Remove the cakes from the pans, and return them, top side up, to the rack to cool completely.

Place one layer on a plate or cake stand. Frost the top with about one-third of the Cream Cheese Frosting. Place the second layer on top, and frost the top and sides of the cake. Decorate the sides of the cake with the small sliced strawberries, if using.

1¾ cups fresh or frozen strawberries, thawed and drained (divided, 1½ cups whole, ¼ cup sliced) (240g + 40g)

2 tablespoons water

1½ cups all-purpose flour (180g)

3 tablespoons cornstarch (22g)

1½ teaspoons baking powder

¾ teaspoon salt

7 tablespoons unsalted butter, softened (98g)

1¼ cups sugar (248g)

3 egg whites, room temperature

¾ cup whole milk, room temperature (170g)

1 teaspoon vanilla extract

Cream Cheese Frosting, double recipe (page 144)

Small fresh strawberries, sliced, optional

tiny texas sheet cake

SERVES 9

The perennial potluck favorite delicately laced with cinnamon, Texas Sheet Cake is normally made in a jellyroll pan. Here it's a bit thicker, made in an 8-inch square cake pan.

. . . .

Preheat the oven to 350°F (180°C). Grease an 8-inch square cake pan, and dust with cocoa powder.

Place the butter, cocoa, and water in a small saucepan. Bring to a boil over medium heat. Remove from the heat, and let cool slightly.

Whisk together the flour, sugar, baking soda, salt, and cinnamon in a medium bowl. Add the chocolate mixture, and whisk until blended. Add the buttermilk, egg, and vanilla, and whisk until blended. Scrape the batter into the prepared pan, and smooth the top.

Bake the cake 20 to 25 minutes, until a tester inserted in the center comes out almost clean. Place the pan on a wire rack, and let the cake cool.

To prepare the topping, whisk together the egg yolks, milk, sugar, and butter in a small saucepan. Bring to a boil over medium-high heat. Reduce the heat to medium, and cook, stirring constantly, until thick, about 8 minutes. Remove from the heat, and stir in the vanilla, pecans, and coconut. Let cool about 15 minutes, then spread on top of the cake while still in the pan.

cake

½ cup unsalted butter (110g)

3 tablespoons unsweetened cocoa powder (23g)

½ cup water

1 cup all-purpose flour (120g)

1 cup sugar (198g)

½ teaspoon baking soda

½ teaspoon salt

½ teaspoon ground cinnamon

½ cup buttermilk, room temperature (113g)

1 egg, room temperature, slightly beaten

½ teaspoon vanilla extract

topping

2 egg yolks

⅔ cup whole milk

⅔ cup sugar

2 tablespoons unsalted butter

½ teaspoon salt

1 teaspoon vanilla extract

½ cup chopped pecans

½ cup sweetened flaked coconut

vanilla sponge cake

with PINEAPPLE FILLING AND CARAMEL FROSTING

SERVES 8

A tender, delicate cake, this beauty reaches glorious heights with its pineapple filling and homemade Caramel Frosting.

Preheat the oven to 350°F (180°C). Grease two 6-inch round cake pans. Line the pans with parchment paper. Grease the parchment. Dust the pans with flour.

Place a mixing bowl over a pan of simmering water. Add the eggs and sugar, and whisk until blended. Cook until the sugar is completely dissolved and the mixture reaches 115°F (45°C). Using an electric mixer at high speed, beat the egg mixture until it has increased in volume about five times, 7 or 8 minutes. When you raise the beater, the mixture should fall back into the bowl forming a ribbon that sits on top for a few seconds.

Place the milk and butter in a glass measuring cup, and heat in the microwave until the butter melts and the mixture is just about to boil. Add the vanilla.

Sift the flour, baking powder, and salt over the egg mixture, and fold in gently. Remove about a cup of the mixture to a separate bowl, and stir in the hot milk mixture. Add back to the remaining batter, and whisk until blended. Pour the batter into the prepared pans.

Bake the cakes 17 to 20 minutes, until a tester inserted in the center comes out clean, and the cake easily releases from the sides when pulled with your fingertips. Place the pans on a wire rack, and let the cakes cool 10 minutes. Remove the cakes from the pans, and return them, top side up, to the rack to cool completely. While the cakes are on the rack, brush the tops with the reserved pineapple juice.

To frost the cakes, place one layer on a plate or cake stand. Place the pineapple on top. Spread about one-third of the Caramel Frosting on top. Place the second layer on top, and frost the top and sides of the cake.

2 eggs

¾ cup sugar (149g)

½ cup whole milk (114g)

¼ cup unsalted butter (56g)

½ teaspoon vanilla extract

1 cup all-purpose flour (120g)

1 teaspoon baking powder

¼ teaspoon salt

¼ cup canned crushed pineapple in its own juice, drained, juice reserved

Caramel Frosting (page 146)

"yellow" butter cake

SERVES 8

This tender butter cake is made in an 8-inch square pan, cooled, then cut into two rectangles. Fill and frost as you would a full-size layer cake.

. . . .

Preheat the oven to 350°F (180°C). Grease an 8-inch square cake pan. Line the bottom of the pan with parchment paper. Grease the parchment. Dust the pan with flour.

Whisk together the flour, baking powder, and salt in a medium bowl.

Place the butter in a mixing bowl, and using an electric mixer at medium-high speed, beat until creamy. Add the sugar, and beat until fluffy, about 5 minutes. Add the eggs and egg yolk one at a time, beating well after each addition. Reduce the speed to low, and add the flour mixture and buttermilk a little at a time, beginning and ending with the flour mixture, and beating until just smooth. Add the vanilla, and beat 30 seconds. Scrape into the prepared pan.

Bake the cake 25 to 30 minutes, until beginning to brown and a tester inserted in the center comes out almost clean. Place the pan on a wire rack, and let the cake cool 10 minutes. Remove the cake from the pan, and return it, top side up, to the rack to cool completely.

Cut the cake into two rectangles. Top one with about a quarter of the frosting. Place the second layer on top, and frost the top and sides with the remaining frosting.

1½ cups all-purpose flour (180g)

1½ teaspoons baking powder

¼ teaspoon salt

½ cup unsalted butter, softened (113g)

1 cup sugar (198g)

2 whole eggs, room temperature

1 egg yolk, room temperature

¾ cup buttermilk, room temperature (169g)

1½ teaspoon vanilla extract

Chocolate Ganache (page 150) or Easy Chocolate Buttercream Frosting (page 148)

4

topsy, turvy & tipsy

Upside down cakes are wonderful surprises of sweet or tart fruit, all packaged in a delicately flavored cake. Made in a regular round cake pan or a cast-iron skillet, they're simple to assemble and a delight to unmold and serve. That's when their glistening fruit topping shows off to perfection.

Tipsy cakes get their kick from small amounts of liquor or liqueur. Their icing is often flavored with an alcoholic libation as well. Perfect for parties and celebrations of all kinds, these spirited confections can be lightly or heavily doused with liquor. Start with a small amount (2 tablespoons of hard liquor or 4 tablespoons of liqueur) and work your way up to your taste (¾ cup of either liquor or liqueur).

blackberry-almond upside down cake

SERVES 8

A smattering of confectioner's sugar brings this fruity beauty to life. Leftovers are great for breakfast.

Preheat the oven to 350°F (180°C). Grease an 8-inch round cake pan. Line with parchment paper. Grease the parchment. Dust the pan with flour.

Place the berries in a small bowl. Sprinkle 1½ tablespoons (19g) of the granulated sugar on top, and toss to coat the berries. Place the berries in a single layer in the pan.

Whisk together the flour, baking powder, baking soda, and salt in a medium bowl.

Whisk together the milk and yogurt in a small bowl.

Place the butter in a mixing bowl. Using an electric mixer at medium-high speed, beat until creamy. Add the remaining 1 cup of the granulated sugar, and beat until fluffy, about 4 minutes. Add the eggs and egg yolk one at a time, beating well after each addition. Reduce the speed to low, and add the flour mixture and the yogurt mixture a little at a time, beginning and ending with the flour mixture. Beat until just blended. Add the vanilla and almond extracts, and beat 30 seconds. Add the almonds, and beat until blended. Using a large spoon, dollop the batter over the berries, taking care not to move the berries too much. Smooth the top.

Bake the cake 40 to 45 minutes, until a tester inserted in the center comes out clean. Place the pan on a wire rack, and let the cake cool 15 minutes. Place a large plate over the cake, and invert the pan to release the cake. Place the plate on a wire rack, and let the cake cool completely. Dust with confectioner's sugar.

6 ounces fresh blackberries

1 cup plus 1½ tablespoons granulated sugar, divided (198g + 19g)

1⅔ cups all-purpose flour (200g)

1 teaspoon baking powder

½ teaspoon baking soda

½ teaspoon salt

¼ cup whole milk, room temperature (56g)

½ cup plain yogurt, room temperature (112g)

9 tablespoons unsalted butter, softened (126g)

2 eggs, room temperature

1 egg yolk, room temperature

1 teaspoon vanilla extract

½ teaspoon almond extract

½ cup finely ground slivered almonds

Confectioner's sugar

peach or mango upside down cake

SERVES 8

You can use fresh or frozen fruit in this tender cake. Just be sure to thaw frozen fruit in a colander to drain off the excess liquid.

Heat ¼ cup (56g) of the butter and the brown sugar in a 9-inch cast-iron skillet over medium heat. When bubbling, add the fruit in a single layer, and cook 5 minutes. Remove from the heat.

Preheat the oven to 350°F (180°C).

Whisk together the flour, baking powder, and salt in a medium bowl.

Place the remaining ½ cup (113g) of the butter in a mixing bowl, and using an electric mixer at medium-high speed, beat until creamy. Add the granulated sugar, and beat until fluffy, about 4 minutes. Add the eggs one at a time, beating well after each addition. Reduce the speed to low, and add the flour mixture and yogurt a little at a time, beginning and ending with the flour mixture. Beat until just smooth. Add the vanilla, and beat 30 seconds. Using a large spoon, dollop the batter over the fruit. Smooth the top.

Bake the cake 30 to 35 minutes, until the top is golden brown. You may want to place a baking sheet on the rack below the cake to catch any drips. Place the pan on a wire rack, and let the cake cool 20 minutes. Place a large plate over the cake. Invert the pan to release the cake. Place the plate on a wire rack, and let the cake cool completely.

¾ cup unsalted butter, softened, divided (144g)

⅓ cup packed light brown sugar (71g)

2 cups sliced peaches or ½-inch cubes mango

1½ cups all-purpose flour (180g)

1 teaspoon baking powder

½ teaspoon salt

1 cup granulated sugar (198g)

3 eggs, room temperature

¼ cup plain yogurt, room temperature (61g)

1 teaspoon vanilla extract

chocolate whiskey cream cake

SERVES 9

Use a whiskey cream liqueur, such as Bailey's Irish Cream or Whisper Creek Tennessee Sipping Cream, in this rich chocolate cake.

. . . .

Preheat the oven to 350°F (180°C). Grease an 8-inch square cake pan. Line with parchment paper. Grease the parchment. Dust the pan with cocoa powder.

Whisk together the flour, cocoa, baking soda, and salt in a small bowl.

Whisk together the whiskey cream and coffee in a small bowl.

Place the egg and sugar in a mixing bowl, and using an electric mixer at medium speed, beat until smooth, about 2 minutes. Add the oil and yogurt, and beat until well combined. Reduce the speed to low, and add the flour mixture and the whiskey cream mixture a little at a time, beginning and ending with the flour mixture. Pour the batter into the prepared pan.

Bake the cake 20 to 22 minutes, until a tester inserted in the center comes out clean. Place the pan on a wire rack, and let the cake cool 10 minutes. Remove the cake from the pan, and return it, top side up, to the rack to cool completely.

To prepare the frosting, beat the butter until smooth. Add the confectioner's sugar a little at a time, beating until smooth. Add the whiskey cream, and beat until blended. Spread the frosting on top of the cake.

cake

1¼ cups all-purpose flour (150g)

6 tablespoons unsweetened cocoa (45g)

1¼ teaspoons baking soda

¼ teaspoon salt

3 tablespoons whiskey cream liqueur

½ cup strong-brewed coffee, room temperature (112g)

1 egg, room temperature

1 cup granulated sugar (198g)

⅓ cup canola oil (66g)

6 tablespoons plain yogurt, room temperature (91g)

whiskey buttercream

⅓ cup butter, softened

1½ cups confectioner's sugar

2 tablespoons whiskey cream liqueur

chocolate jack cake

SERVES 8

With its spike of whiskey and handful of chocolate chips, this cake is one that those who love their Tennessee whiskey will adore.

Preheat the oven to 350°F (180°C). Grease an 8-inch round cake pan. Line with parchment paper. Grease the parchment. Dust the pan with cocoa.

Whisk together the flour, baking soda, salt, and black pepper.

Whisk together the coffee, whiskey, and vanilla in a measuring cup.

Combine the sugars and cocoa in a small bowl.

Place the butter in a mixing bowl, and using an electric mixer at medium-high speed, beat until creamy. Reduce the speed to low, and add the cocoa mixture. Beat until smooth, about 3 minutes, increasing the speed to medium as the mixture comes together. Add the eggs, one at a time, beating well after each addition. Reduce the speed to low, and add the flour mixture and whiskey mixture a little at a time, beginning and ending with the flour mixture. Beat until just combined. Fold in the chocolate chips. Scrape the batter into the prepared pan.

Bake the cake 23 to 28 minutes, until a tester inserted in the center comes out almost clean. The top will be cracked. Place the pan on a wire rack, and let the cake cool 10 minutes. Remove the cake from the pan, and return it, top side up, to the rack to cool completely. The cake will fall slightly in the middle. Serve warm, while the chips are still molten, with Sweetened Whipped Cream.

1½ cups all-purpose flour (180g)

1 teaspoon baking soda

½ teaspoon salt

¼ teaspoon black pepper

½ cup strong-brewed coffee, cooled (112g)

3 tablespoons whiskey, such as Jack Daniel's (42g)

1 teaspoon vanilla extract

½ cup granulated sugar (99g)

1 cup packed brown sugar (107g)

½ cup unsweetened cocoa powder (60g)

7 tablespoons unsalted butter, softened (98g)

2 eggs, room temperature

½ cup mini semisweet chocolate chips

Sweetened Whipped Cream (page 151)

pina colada cake

SERVES 8

*J*ust enough for a small birthday celebration, this cake showcases toasted coconut and rum. Toast the coconut flakes on a baking sheet in a 350°F (180°C) oven until brown—but watch carefully. They can go from white to burned in a flash. Shake the can of coconut milk really well, and after opening the can, stir the thickened coconut cream into the thinner milk until smooth.

Preheat the oven to 350°F (180°C). Grease an 8-inch round cake pan. Line with parchment paper. Grease the parchment. Dust the pan with flour.

Whisk together the flour, baking powder, and salt in a small bowl.

Combine the coconut oil, vanilla, and coconut milk in a measuring cup, and stir well.

Place the butter in a mixing bowl, and using an electric mixer at medium-high speed, beat until creamy. Add the granulated sugar, and beat until fluffy, about 4 minutes. Add the eggs one at a time, beating well after each addition. Reduce the speed to low, and add the flour mixture and the coconut milk mixture a little at a time, beginning and ending with the flour mixture. Fold in the coconut. Scrape the batter into the prepared pan.

Bake the cake 18 to 20 minutes, until a tester inserted in the center comes out clean. Place the pan on a wire rack, and let the cake cool 10 minutes. Remove the cake from the pan, and return it, top side up, to the rack set over a baking sheet to catch drips.

To prepare the glaze, whisk together the pineapple juice, lime peel, lime juice, rum, and granulated sugar until the sugar dissolves. Poke holes in the warm cake with a fork or skewer, and spoon the glaze over the top of the cake.

To prepare the whipped cream, whip the cream until soft peaks form. Add the vanilla, lime peel, and confectioner's sugar, and whip until the desired consistency is reached. Slice the cake into wedges, and serve with the whipped cream.

cake

1 cup all-purpose flour (120g)

½ teaspoon baking powder

¼ teaspoon salt

2 tablespoons coconut oil, melted and slightly cooled (24g)

½ teaspoon vanilla extract

¼ cup unsweetened coconut milk (56g)

⅓ cup unsalted butter, softened (75g)

⅔ cup granulated sugar (131g)

2 eggs, room temperature

⅔ cup unsweetened coconut flakes, toasted

glaze

1 tablespoon pineapple juice

½ tablespoon finely grated lime peel

1 tablespoon fresh lime juice

2 tablespoons white or dark rum

1 tablespoon granulated sugar

lime whipped cream

1 cup whipping cream

¼ teaspoon vanilla extract

1½ teaspoons finely grated lime peel

2 tablespoons confectioner's sugar

rum cake

with GLAZED PECAN TOPPING

SERVES 9

Lots of rum cake recipes call for a box of instant vanilla pudding. This recipe makes a super tender cake without the processed ingredients.

Preheat the oven to 350°F (180°C). Grease an 8-inch round cake pan. Line with parchment paper. Grease the parchment. Dust the pan with flour.

To prepare the cake, whisk together the flour, baking powder, and salt in a small bowl.

Whisk together the milk, rum, and vanilla in a measuring cup.

Place the butter in a mixing bowl, and using an electric mixer at medium-high speed, beat until creamy. Add the sugars, and beat until fluffy, about 4 minutes. Add the eggs and egg yolk one at a time, beating well after each addition. Reduce the speed to low, and add the flour mixture and the milk mixture a little at a time, beginning and ending with the flour mixture. Beat until just smooth. Scrape the batter into the prepared pan.

Bake the cake 25 to 30 minutes, until a tester inserted in the center comes out clean. Place the pan on a wire rack, and let the cake cool 10 minutes. Remove from the pan, and return it, top side up, to the rack to cool completely.

To prepare the topping, combine the sugar, butter, corn syrup, and salt in a small saucepan. Cook over medium heat, stirring constantly, until the mixture reaches 240°F (115°C, soft ball stage). Remove from heat. Stir in the rum until smooth. Stir in the pecans. Let cool slightly, about 5 minutes, then pour over the cooled cake. Spread the topping to the edges.

cake

1¼ cups all-purpose flour (150g)

1 teaspoon baking powder

¼ teaspoon salt

¼ cup whole milk, room temperature (56g)

2 tablespoons white or dark rum

¾ teaspoon vanilla extract

½ cup unsalted butter, softened (113g)

½ cup packed brown sugar (106g)

¼ cup granulated sugar (50g)

2 eggs, room temperature

1 egg yolk, room temperature

topping

½ cup packed brown sugar

4 tablespoons butter

1 tablespoon light corn syrup

½ teaspoon salt

2 tablespoons rum

½ cup chopped pecans, toasted

kahlua cake

SERVES 8

*C*offee and chocolate combine in this moist cake. To make this cake even more festive, cut each of the two layers in half horizontally, and fill and frost the four layers.

Preheat the oven to 350°F (180°C). Grease two 6-inch cake pans. Line the pans with parchment paper. Grease the parchment. Dust the pans with cocoa powder.

Combine the flour, baking soda, and salt in a small bowl.

Combine the liqueur, coffee, and buttermilk in a small bowl.

Place the butter in a mixing bowl, and using an electric mixer at medium-high speed, beat until creamy. Add the granulated sugar, and beat until fluffy, about 4 minutes. Add the cocoa, and beat until combined. Add the eggs one at a time, beating well after each addition. Reduce the speed to low, and add the flour mixture and the buttermilk mixture a little at a time, beginning and ending with the flour mixture. Beat until just smooth. Scrape the batter into the prepared pans.

Bake the cakes 25 to 30 minutes, until a tester inserted in the center comes out clean. Place the pans on a wire rack, and let the cakes cool 10 minutes. Remove the cakes from the pans, and return them, top side up, to the rack to cool completely.

To prepare the frosting, place the butter in a mixing bowl. Using an electric mixer at medium speed, beat until creamy. Add the confectioner's sugar a little at a time, and beat until smooth. Add the coffee liqueur, a tablespoon at a time, beating until the frosting reaches the desired consistency. Add more sugar for a thicker frosting, or more liqueur for a thinner frosting.

Place one layer on a plate or cake stand. Top one with about a quarter of the frosting. Place the second layer on top, and frost the top and sides with the remaining frosting. Or cut the layers in half horizontally to form four layers, and frost only the tops of each layer.

cake

1¼ cups all-purpose flour (150g)

1 teaspoon baking soda

¼ teaspoon salt

5 tablespoons coffee-flavored liqueur, such as Kahlua (89g)

3 tablespoons strong-brewed coffee, cooled (43g)

6 tablespoons buttermilk (84g)

7 tablespoons butter, softened (98g)

1¼ cups granulated sugar (248g)

7 tablespoons unsweetened cocoa (53g)

2 eggs, room temperature

kahlua buttercream frosting

½ cup butter, softened

2 cups confectioner's sugar

¼ cup coffee-flavored liqueur, such as Kahlua

5

let them eat cake...
for breakfast

Perfect for brunches or holiday breakfasts, these cakes are an eye-opening start to a perfect day. You can make them a day ahead, wrap them well in foil, and refrigerate overnight. Bring them to room temperature before serving.

oatmeal-applesauce cake

with LEMONY APPLE TOPPING

SERVES 9

The oats in this cake give it a bit of a chewy texture. Make a double batch of the apple topping, and save it (refrigerated) for serving with vanilla ice cream or pancakes.

Preheat the oven to 350°F (180°C). Grease an 8-inch square cake pan. Dust with flour.

Whisk together the flour, baking powder, salt, and cinnamon in a small bowl.

Place the butter in a mixing bowl. Using an electric mixer at medium-high speed, beat until creamy. Add the sugar, and beat until fluffy, about 4 minutes. Add the egg and egg yolk one at a time, beating well after each addition. Reduce the speed to low, and add the oats, beating until blended. Add the flour mixture and the applesauce a little at a time, beginning and ending with the flour mixture. Add the vanilla, and beat for 30 seconds. Scrape the batter into the prepared pan.

Bake the cake 25 to 30 minutes, until a tester inserted in the center comes out almost clean. Place the pan on a wire rack, and let the cake cool completely.

To prepare the topping, combine the apples, lemon juice, sugar, cinnamon, and water in a small saucepan. Bring to a boil over medium-high heat. Reduce the heat to low, and simmer until the apples are tender, about 10 minutes. Serve the topping warm over the cake.

cake

1 cup plus 2 tablespoons all-purpose flour (135g)

¾ teaspoon baking powder

¼ teaspoon salt

¼ teaspoon ground cinnamon

6 tablespoons unsalted butter, softened (84g)

¾ cup sugar (149g)

1 egg, room temperature

1 egg yolk, room temperature

¾ cup quick-cooking oats (74g)

1 cup unsweetened applesauce (244g)

¾ teaspoon vanilla extract

topping

2 tart-sweet apples, such as Honey Crisp, peeled, cored, and cut into eighths

2 tablespoons lemon juice

½ cup sugar

1 teaspoon cinnamon

¼ cup water

blackberry-almond coffee cake

SERVES 8

Fresh blackberries star in this moist cake, making it perfect for breakfast or afternoon tea.

Preheat the oven to 350°F (180°C). Grease an 8-inch round cake pan. Dust with flour.

To prepare the topping, combine the flour, brown sugar, butter, chopped almonds, and salt in a small bowl. Using your fingers, press the butter into the mixture until crumbs form.

To prepare the cake, place the blackberries in a small bowl. Add 2 teaspoons of the flour (7g) and 1 tablespoon of the granulated sugar (12g), and toss to coat.

Whisk together the remaining 1 cup of the flour (120g), baking powder, baking soda, and salt in a small bowl.

Place the butter in a mixing bowl. Using an electric mixer at medium-high speed, beat until creamy. Add the remaining ¾ cup of the sugar (150g), and beat until fluffy, about 5 minutes. Add the egg, and beat well. Reduce the speed to low, and add the flour mixture and the buttermilk a little at a time, beginning and ending with the flour mixture. Add the vanilla extract and the almond extract, and beat 30 seconds. Scrape half the batter into the prepared pan. Place the blackberries on top. Dollop the remaining batter over the berries, and smooth it to the edge, taking care to keep the berries away from the side of the pan. The batter will barely cover the berries. Scatter the topping crumbs over the top of the batter.

Bake the cake 35 to 40 minutes, until a tester inserted in the center comes out almost clean. Place the pan on a wire rack, and let the cake cool completely.

topping

¼ cup all-purpose flour

2 tablespoons brown sugar

3 tablespoons unsalted butter, softened

½ cup chopped slivered almonds

½ teaspoon salt

cake

1 cup blackberries

1 cup plus 2 teaspoons all-purpose flour, divided (120g + 7g)

¾ cup plus 1 tablespoon granulated sugar, divided (150g + 12g)

½ teaspoon baking powder

¼ teaspoon baking soda

¼ teaspoon salt

¼ cup unsalted butter (56g)

1 egg, room temperature

½ cup buttermilk, room temperature (113g)

¼ teaspoon vanilla extract

¼ teaspoon almond extract

cranberry-walnut coffee cake

SERVES 8

*D*ried cranberries and walnuts give this cake a festive holiday appeal.

Preheat the oven to 350°F (180°C). Grease an 8-inch round cake pan. Dust with flour.

To prepare the streusel, combine butter, brown sugar, and flour in a medium bowl. Using a pastry blender or two knives, cut in the butter until the mixture resembles small peas. Set aside.

To prepare the cake, place the cranberries and walnuts in a small bowl. Add 1 tablespoon of the flour, and toss to coat.

Whisk together the remaining flour, baking powder, baking soda, and salt in a small bowl.

Place the butter in a mixing bowl. Using an electric mixer at medium-high speed, beat until creamy. Add the granulated sugar, and beat until fluffy, about 5 minutes. Add the egg, and beat well. Reduce the speed to low, and add the flour mixture and the sour cream a little at a time, beginning and ending with the flour mixture. Add the orange peel, and beat 30 seconds. Fold in the cranberries and walnuts. Scrape the batter into the prepared pan. Sprinkle the streusel over the cake batter.

Bake the cake 30 to 35 minutes, until a tester inserted in the center comes out almost clean. Place the pan on a wire rack, and let the cake cool completely.

streusel

3 tablespoons cold, unsalted butter, cut into small pieces

2 tablespoons brown sugar

¼ cup all-purpose flour

cake

½ cup dried cranberries

½ cup chopped walnuts

1 cup all-purpose flour (120g), divided

¾ teaspoon baking powder

½ teaspoon baking soda

¼ teaspoon salt

¼ cup unsalted butter (56g)

10 tablespoons granulated sugar (124g)

1 egg, room temperature

10 tablespoons sour cream, room temperature (152g)

½ teaspoon finely grated orange peel

orange marmalade loaf

with COCONUT TOPPING

SERVES 8

The sweet cake is perfect with a cup of tea. The coconut topping sinks into the cake as it bakes.

Preheat the oven to 350°F (180°C). Grease an 8½ by 4½-inch loaf pan. Line the pan with parchment paper, bringing the paper up and over the long sides of the pan. Grease the parchment. Dust the pan with flour.

To prepare the topping, combine the sugar and flour in a small bowl. Add the butter, and using a pastry blender or two knives, cut in the butter until the mixture resembles small peas. Add the coconut flakes, and blend in with the pastry cutter.

To prepare the cake, whisk together the flour, baking powder, and salt in a small bowl.

Place the butter in a mixing bowl. Using an electric mixer at medium-high speed, beat until creamy. Add the sugar, and beat until fluffy, about 4 minutes. Add the eggs one at a time, beating well after each addition. Reduce the speed to low, and add the flour mixture and the orange juice a little at a time, beginning and ending with the flour mixture. Beat until just blended. Add the marmalade and orange peel, and beat until blended. Scrape the batter into the prepared pan. Sprinkle the topping over the batter.

Bake the cake 35 to 38 minutes, until a tester inserted in the center comes out clean. Place the pan on a wire rack, and let the cake cool 10 minutes. Remove the cake from the pan, and return it, top side up, to the rack to cool completely.

topping

2 tablespoons sugar

2 tablespoons all-purpose flour

1 tablespoon cold butter, cut into small pieces

3 tablespoons unsweetened coconut flakes

cake

1 cup all-purpose flour (120g)

1 teaspoon baking powder

½ teaspoon salt

½ cup unsalted butter, softened (113g)

⅔ cup sugar (131g)

3 eggs, room temperature

¼ cup fresh orange juice

¼ cup orange marmalade

½ teaspoon finely grated orange peel

crumb cake

SERVES 9

Topped with a thick layer of buttery crumbs, this cake does double duty as a breakfast cake and lunchtime dessert.

Preheat the oven to 350°F (180°C). Grease an 8-inch square baking pan.

To prepare the topping, combine the flour, salt, vanilla, brown sugar, and cinnamon in a medium bowl. Pour the melted butter over all, and fluff to form coarse crumbs. Set aside.

To prepare the cake, whisk together the flour, baking soda, salt, and nutmeg in a medium bowl.

Place the butter in a mixing bowl, and beat with an electric mixer at medium-high speed until creamy. Add the sugars, and beat until fluffy, about 5 minutes. Add the eggs one at a time, and beat until smooth. Reduce the speed to low, and add the flour mixture and buttermilk a little at a time, beginning and ending with the flour mixture. Beat until just combined. Add the vanilla, and beat 30 seconds. Scrape the batter into the prepared pan.

Using your fingers, crumble the crumb mixture over the batter, covering it completely. Gently pat the crumbs.

Bake the cake 35 minutes, or until a tester inserted in the center comes out clean. Place the pan on a wire rack, and let the cake cool completely.

topping

1½ cups all-purpose flour (180g)

¼ teaspoon salt

¼ teaspoon vanilla extract

1 cup packed brown sugar (213g)

1 teaspoon ground cinnamon

½ cup unsalted butter, melted

cake

1½ cups all-purpose flour (180g)

½ teaspoon baking soda

¾ teaspoon salt

½ teaspoon ground nutmeg

7 tablespoons unsalted butter, softened (96g)

½ cup granulated sugar (99g)

½ cup packed brown sugar (106g)

2 eggs, room temperature

½ cup buttermilk (113g)

1 teaspoon vanilla extract

sour cream coffee cake

with COCONUT STREUSEL

Make this cake the night before you plan to serve it for breakfast or brunch. It's not too sweet, making it perfect for a morning treat.

Preheat the oven to 350°F (180°C). Grease an 8-inch square cake pan. Dust with flour.

To prepare the streusel, combine the brown sugar, flour, salt, cinnamon, and nutmeg in a medium bowl. Pour in the melted butter, and stir with a fork to blend. Add the coconut, and stir well.

To prepare the cake, whisk together the flour, baking powder, baking soda, and salt in a medium bowl.

Place the butter in a mixing bowl. Using an electric mixer at medium-high speed, beat until creamy. Add the granulated sugar, and beat until fluffy, about 4 minutes. Add the eggs one at a time, beating well after each addition. Reduce the speed to low, and add the flour mixture and the sour cream a little at a time, beginning and ending with the flour mixture. Beat until just smooth. Add the vanilla and lemon peel, and beat 30 seconds. Scrape half the batter into the prepared pan. Evenly sprinkle half the streusel on top. Scrape the remaining batter on top. Smooth the top, and evenly top with the remaining streusel.

Bake the cake 35 to 40 minutes, until a tester inserted in the center comes out clean. Place the pan on a wire rack, and let the cake cool completely.

streusel

½ cup packed light brown sugar (106g)

½ cup all-purpose flour (60g)

¼ teaspoon salt

½ teaspoon ground cinnamon

¼ teaspoon ground nutmeg

¼ cup unsalted butter, melted

⅔ cup unsweetened shredded coconut or coconut flakes

cake

1½ cups all-purpose flour (180g)

¾ teaspoon baking powder

¾ teaspoon baking soda

¼ teaspoon salt

½ cup unsalted butter, softened (113g)

1 cup granulated sugar (198g)

2 eggs, room temperature

1 cup sour cream (243g)

1 teaspoon vanilla extract

1 teaspoon finely grated lemon peel

glazes, sauces & more

These creamy frostings and sweet glazes will be your go-to recipes for any number of cakes. Mix and match as you desire, or add your own special touches to them to give them a different main flavor.

cream cheese frosting

MAKES ABOUT 1¼ CUPS

Basic cream cheese frosting can be flavored in a number of ways: Add a tablespoon of pineapple juice from a can of drained crushed pineapple; for Lime Cream Cheese Frosting (used on page 80), add 2 tablespoons fresh lime juice and increase the sugar to 2 cups.

Combine the cream cheese and butter in a mixing bowl, and beat with a hand mixer until blended. Add the confectioner's sugar a little at a time, beating until blended. Add the vanilla and salt, and beat until blended. If the mixture is too thick, add a teaspoon or two of milk. If you want a thicker frosting, add more confectioner's sugar.

4 ounces cream cheese, softened

3 tablespoons unsalted butter, softened

1½ cups confectioner's sugar

½ teaspoon vanilla extract

¼ teaspoon salt

butter sauce

MAKES ABOUT 1½ CUPS

Combine the butter, sugars, cornstarch, salt, and water in a saucepan. Bring to a boil over medium heat, and cook until dark amber, about 5 minutes. Remove from the heat, and let cool slightly. Stir in the vanilla.

6 tablespoons unsalted butter

½ cup granulated sugar

½ cup packed brown sugar

1 tablespoon cornstarch

¼ teaspoon salt

1 cup water

½ teaspoon vanilla extract

chocolate glaze — two ways

MAKES ABOUT 1 CUP

Both versions make a glaze that's smooth and thin enough to drizzle using the tines of a fork. If you prefer to spoon it on, let the glaze cool slightly until barely thickened.

For the cream version, place chopped chocolate in a bowl. In a small saucepan, heat the heavy cream to a simmer. Pour the cream over the chocolate, and stir until the chocolate is melted and the mixture is smooth. Stir in the vanilla and salt.

For the butter version, place the chopped chocolate, butter, and corn syrup in the top of a double boiler. Heat over barely simmering water, stirring occasionally, until the chocolate is melted. Stir in the vanilla and salt.

cream version

1 cup chopped chocolate

½ cup heavy cream

1 teaspoon vanilla extract

⅛ teaspoon salt

butter version

¾ cup chopped chocolate

3 tablespoons unsalted butter

1 tablespoon corn syrup

1 teaspoon vanilla extract

⅛ teaspoon salt

lemon butter sauce

MAKES ABOUT 1 CUP

Combine the butter, sugar, cornstarch, and milk in a saucepan. Bring to a boil over medium-high heat, and boil for 2 minutes, stirring constantly. Remove from the heat, and stir in the lemon juice and vanilla.

⅓ cup unsalted butter

1 cup sugar

1 tablespoon cornstarch

½ cup evaporated milk

2 teaspoons lemon juice

1 teaspoon vanilla extract

caramel frosting

MAKES ABOUT 3 CUPS

Use this decadent frosting on Jam Cake (page 40) and Vanilla Sponge Cake with Pineapple Filling (page 108).

Combine 2 cups of the sugar with the butter, baking soda, and heavy cream in a small saucepan. Heat over medium until the mixture comes to a low boil. Remove from heat, and cover to keep warm.

Place the remaining ½ cup sugar in a medium nonstick skillet. Heat over medium-high heat until the sugar melts, stirring frequently. Continue to cook the sugar until it turns dark amber, stirring constantly. Reduce the heat to low, and slowly pour in the cream mixture. The caramel will sputter and sizzle. Cook while stirring until the mixture reaches 240°F (115°C, soft ball stage). Remove from the heat, and let cool slightly. Transfer the caramel to a mixing bowl. Using an electric mixer fitted with a whisk attachment, beat the frosting until it reaches a spreadable consistency, about 6 minutes for a full recipe or 4 minutes for a half recipe. Beat in the salt. If the frosting becomes too hard to spread easily, heat a few tablespoons of heavy cream in the microwave, and drizzle the cream over the frosting. Stir until well blended.

2½ cups sugar, divided

3 tablespoons unsalted butter

¼ teaspoon baking soda

1 cup heavy cream

½ teaspoon salt

easy chocolate buttercream frosting

MAKES ABOUT 2 CUPS

Combine the butter and cocoa in a mixing bowl. Using an electric mixer at medium speed, beat until blended. Add the heavy cream and vanilla, and beat until blended. Add the confectioner's sugar a little at a time, beating until the desired consistency is reached. Beat in the salt.

6 tablespoons unsalted butter, softened

½ cup unsweetened cocoa powder

½ cup heavy cream

1½ teaspoons vanilla extract

2 to 2½ cups confectioner's sugar

½ teaspoon salt

peanut butter frosting

MAKES ABOUT 1 CUP

Combine the butter, peanut butter, honey, salt, and vanilla in a mixing bowl. Using an electric mixer at medium speed, beat until blended. Add the confectioner's sugar a little at a time, and beat until smooth.

¼ cup unsalted butter

¼ cup creamy peanut butter (not natural)

1 tablespoon honey

¼ teaspoon salt

½ teaspoon vanilla extract

¾ cup confectioner's sugar

raspberry wine coulis

MAKES ABOUT 2 CUPS

Combine the sugar, raspberries, water, and wine in a small saucepan over medium-high heat. Bring to a boil. Reduce the heat, and cook until the sugar is dissolved, about 6 minutes. Let cool.

Pour the mixture into the bowl of a food processor and process until smooth. Pour the puree through a wire mesh sieve to remove the seeds. Chill. Serve the sauce spooned alongside or over servings of cake.

¾ cup sugar

3 cups raspberries

¼ cup water

¼ cup dry rosé wine

fudgy chocolate sauce

MAKES ABOUT 2 CUPS

This sauce is from a friend of my husband's family. I like to keep it on hand to serve with One Egg Dinner Cake (page 24) or ice cream. It's hard to resist eating it with a spoon directly from the jar.

Melt the butter and chocolate in a double boiler set over simmering water. Add the remaining ingredients, and cook, stirring occasionally, about 20 minutes. Spoon into a clean 1-pint jar with a lid. Let cool, then store in the refrigerator.

To reheat, set the glass jar in a pot of barely simmering water over very low heat until chocolate has thinned to sauce consistency. Stir well. The sauce can be reheated as often as needed.

½ cup unsalted butter

4 ounces unsweetened chocolate, chopped

3 cups sugar

½ teaspoon salt

2 teaspoons vanilla extract

12 ounces evaporated milk

chocolate ganache

MAKES ABOUT 3 CUPS

Use Chocolate Ganache to frost the Siren's Chocolate Cake (page 92) and the "Yellow" Butter Cake (page 110). Use the Mexican variation for the Mexican Chocolate Cake (page 94).

8 ounces semisweet
   chocolate chips

1½ cups heavy cream

1 teaspoon vanilla extract

Place the chocolate chips in a mixing bowl. Heat the cream in a small saucepan until small bubbles begin to appear around the edges. Pour the cream over the chips, and let stand about 10 minutes. Stir the mixture until the chips are completely melted and the mixture is smooth. Let cool completely. (You can refrigerate the mixture to speed up the cooling.) Using a stand mixer fitted with a whisk attachment, beat the mixture on high speed until fluffy. Beat in the vanilla.

mexican variation

Add 2 tablespoons coffee liqueur, such as Kahlua, ¼ teaspoon ground cinnamon, and a dash of cayenne pepper to the chips before adding the heated cream.

chocolate cream cheese frosting

MAKES ABOUT 2 CUPS

Place the chocolate chips in a glass measuring cup, and microwave in 30-second increments, stirring between each, until melted and smooth.

Combine the confectioner's sugar, cocoa, and salt in a medium bowl.

Combine the cream cheese and butter in a mixing bowl. Using an electric mixer at medium speed, beat until smooth and blended. Add the cocoa mixture, and beat until blended. Add the melted chocolate and sour cream, and beat until smooth.

6 ounces bittersweet chocolate chips

1½ cups confectioner's sugar

3 tablespoons unsweetened cocoa powder

¼ teaspoon salt

4 ounces cream cheese, softened

¼ cup unsalted butter, softened

½ cup sour cream

sweetened whipped cream

MAKES ABOUT 1½ TO CUPS

Homemade whipped cream is about as easy a recipe as there is, so why buy premade whipped topping? There's no comparison in taste and creaminess. Use as much or as little sugar as you like.

Pour the cold heavy cream into a chilled bowl. Using beaters that have been chilled, beat with a handheld electric mixer until soft peaks form. Gradually add the confectioner's sugar, and beat until the desired consistency is reached. Add the vanilla, and beat until blended.

1 cup cold heavy whipping cream

2 to 4 tablespoons confectioner's sugar

1 teaspoon vanilla extract

appendix

resources

These are the items used in preparing the recipes for this book. They can be found at your favorite kitchen retailer or online.

CAKE PANS

Fat Daddio's Anodized Aluminum Cake Pans

Parrish's Magic Line Cake Pans

Wilton Performance Pans

WIRE COOLING RACKS

Hamilton Housewares Stainless Steel Cooling Rack

Nordic Ware Round Cooling Rack

OFFSET SPATULAS

Williams Sonoma 4-inch and 8-inch Offset Icing Spatulas

Ateco Offset Plastic Handle Icing Spatula, 4½-inch or 7¾-inch

CANDY THERMOMETER

(for boiled icings and glazes)

Sur La Table Candy and Deep Fry Thermometer

Taylor Candy/Deep Fry Thermometer

DIGITAL KITCHEN SCALE

Rophie Accurate Digital Scale

Oxo 5-Pound Food Scale

CAKE TESTER

Amish Cake Tester

recipe index

index

Note: Page numbers in *italics* indicate recipe photos.

index *(continued)*

MORE GREAT BOOKS *from*
SPRING HOUSE PRESS

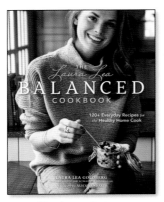

**The Laura Lea
Balanced Cookbook**
978-1940611-56-3
$35.00 | 368 Pages

**Secrets from the
La Varenne Kitchen**
978-1-940611-15-0
$17.95 | 136 Pages

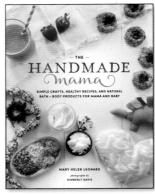

The Handmade Mama
978-1-940611-71-6
$24.95 | 176 Pages

Drink Progressively
978-1940611-58-7
$27.00 | 240 Pages

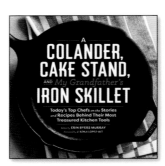

**A Colander, Cake Stand, and
My Grandfather's Iron Skillet**
978-1-940611-36-5
$24.95 | 184 Pages

Fabulous Fat Quarter Aprons
978-1-940611-39-6
$12.99 | 56 pages

SPRING HOUSE PRESS

Look for these Spring House Press titles at your favorite bookstore, specialty retailer,
or visit *www.springhousepress.com.*

For more information about Spring House Press, email us at *info@springhousepress.com.*